the new
persian kitchen

the new
persian kitchen

Louisa Shafia

Photography by Sara Remington

TEN SPEED PRESS

Berkeley

Contents

beverages • 163

pickles and preserves • 175

Introduction

A DESERT PARADISE

I saw a garden pure as paradise . . .
A myriad different hues were mingled there
A myriad scents drenched miles of perfumed air
The rose lay in the hyacinth's embrace
The jasmine nuzzled the carnation's face

—Nezami, *The Haft Paykar (Seven Beauties)*, translation by Julie Scott Meysami

Imagine that you are in a vast desert with the hot sun searing your back. A high stone wall with an elaborate gate appears, and you walk through it. Suddenly you feel cool air on your skin and hear the soft melody of water dancing in a fountain. You are in a lush, blooming garden, and a deep breath brings the honeyed fragrance of roses to your nose. All around you are fruiting trees of pistachios, almonds, walnuts, peaches, apples, pears, sour cherries, and pomegranates. From the ground rise neat rows of squash, cucumber, carrot, eggplant, garlic, and rhubarb. A patch of purple crocus reveals three red saffron stigmas sprouting from each dewy flower, while the scent of limes, turmeric, cardamom, and mint fill the air.

I'm often asked, "So, what exactly *is* Persian food?" The best way I can think of to describe it is as a lush garden in the desert, a familiar image from classical Persian lore. Like our mythical garden, Persian cuisine is perfumed with the floral scents of citrus, rose water, and quince. Indeed, fresh and dried fruits feature in meat, rice, and desserts alike, while ingredients such as pomegranates, saffron, and pistachios are called on as much for their taste as for their striking appearance, which evokes the colors of nature. Why a desert garden? Through a system of underground aquifers, ancient Persians transformed vast stretches of arid land into fertile oases, and over thousands of years, the miracle of water in such unlikely places led to a cuisine that relishes the gifts of the garden in every bite. *The New Persian Kitchen* takes this reverence for fresh food as its starting point, drawing on traditional Persian ingredients and health-conscious cooking

1

techniques, to create a new Persian cuisine that's part contemporary America and part ancient Iran.

The journey of writing this book began a dozen years ago at my first cooking job, at San Francisco's vegan Millennium restaurant, when head chef Eric Tucker asked me to come up with a new entrée. Out of the blue, my first idea was to make the classic Persian dish *fesenjan*, a sweet and tart stew of pomegranate molasses, ground walnuts, and seared chicken or duck. I crafted a meatless version of the dish and enhanced the color with grated red beets. To my delight, the chef and kitchen staff received my creation enthusiastically, and the dish made it onto the menu. Though my father comes from Iran, and I had grown up eating dishes like *fesenjan*, I had simply never given much thought to Persian cooking. Happily, that little push would jump-start my exploration into the food of Iran, and ultimately, into my own Persian heritage.

I grew up in a leafy neighborhood in Philadelphia in the 1970s, a time and place in culinary history marked by a growing enthusiasm for natural foods, contrasting obsessions with Chinese home cooking and Julia Child, and the onset of the "quick weeknight dinner"—a boon to working moms in the form of Ortega tacos, frozen pizza, and canned soup. Our home was influenced by all of these trends, but with a notable difference: there was an otherworldly Persian element in the form of red eggplant stew spiced with pomegranate molasses; fluffy saffron rice; succulent lamb kebabs pulled from hot metal skewers with reams of pillowy flatbread; and a love of fresh fruits like watermelon, oranges, and grapes, all owing to my father's Iranian heritage.

My mother, an Ashkenazi Jew who was born and raised in suburban Philadelphia, and my father, the product of a large Muslim family in Tehran, met while my mom was working as a librarian at the hospital where my dad was an intern. He was late returning books; she called to remind him, and the rest is history. Although my dad had no relatives in the States, and few Persian friends, we did attend grand *Norooz* (Persian New Year) banquets and dinners at the homes of my dad's Persian colleagues. There were also rare visits from our family in Iran, when my dad's sister, my beautiful Aunt Meliheh, would spend days in our kitchen making a feast worthy of Cyrus the Great. Through these experiences, and my mom's impressive attempts to re-create the food of my dad's homeland, the tastes and smells of Persian food were imprinted on my senses.

In the years since, as a culinary professional, I've been drawn to fresh food and healthful cooking, and I've prepared everything from raw to vegan to high-end Swedish food at restaurants in New York and San Francisco. Over time, the allure of my Iranian ancestry has grown stronger, and my passion for produce-centered cooking has been increasingly colored by childhood memories of burbling Persian stews and steaming pyramids of rice. *The New Persian Kitchen* represents the synthesis of those influences and my experience in contemporary cooking.

Obscured for years by a veil of political animosity, Persian food is a global treasure waiting to be discovered. Poised between East and West, Iran boasts a remarkable history that stretches back at least three millennia. Crisscrossed for centuries by intercontinental traders, and at one time extending from North Africa to the Hindu Kush, the Persian Empire was subjugated by both neighboring countries and distant rivals. These many outside influences resulted in a cuisine seasoned by Greeks, Romans, Arabs, Mongols, Turks, Africans, Indians, Chinese, and even Britons and the French. Yet even while embracing new flavors, Persian food has retained its startlingly unique fundamental character.

With the recipes in the following pages, I aim for a similar blending of the foreign and the familiar. Indeed, about half of these recipes are original creations that explore Persian ingredients and cooking techniques in fresh, new ways, while the other half are time-honored dishes that correspond closely enough to the originals to merit including their Persian names.

In general, you'll find that the recipes here emphasize whole grains and gluten-free flours, use minimal amounts of oil and fat, and call for alternatives to white sugar. For readers who want to make the meat dishes without the meat, many of the recipes include a suggestion for how to adapt them to a vegetarian diet.

For kosher cooks looking to avoid mixing meat and dairy, the main dairy ingredient to be aware of in Persian food is yogurt, which is used as an accompaniment to most entrées, and is sometimes cooked right into a dish. Where it's called for in a meat dish, simply leave the yogurt out. Fresh lemon or lime juice, olive oil, or a combination of oil and citrus makes a great substitute. Finally, since Persian cuisine may be unfamiliar to many readers, I've suggested a variety of seasonal menus (see page 186).

My Persian grandfather Yousef was a devoted practitioner of alchemy, the mysterious and ancient science of turning base metals into gold. I'd like to think that his zeal for transformation was handed down to me and manifests in my passion for turning raw ingredients into substances even more delectable and refined than they were in their original form. In the Persian kitchen, our tools are fire and spice, and the secret ingredient is love. With that in mind, I invite you to turn eastward and join me on this adventure into the fairy-tale spices and fantastical fruits of a timeless cuisine. With a warm reverence for the past, and a firm foothold in the present, we'll create our own kitchen alchemy, transmuting fresh ingredients into dazzling feasts.

Overview

PERSIAN CUISINE THROUGH THE AGES

The ingredients for the king's dinner included "sweet grape jelly, candied turnips and radishes prepared with salt, candied capers with salt, from which delicious stuffings are made, terebinth (from pistachio nuts) oil, Ethiopian cumin and Median saffron."

—Polyaenus, *Strategemata*, translation by R. Shepherd

*F*rom very early in their history, Persians have been noted for their extraordinary cuisine. One witness to the delicious details of ancient Persian cooking was Xenophon, the Greek mercenary and eventual historian who fought in the Persian army in 400 BCE. Although disinclined to admire his "barbarian" employers, he had to admit the "superior excellence" of their food, observing that the royal retinue "is always contriving new dishes, as well as sauces, for they have cooks to find out varieties in both." The Persians, he wrote, had dispatched "vintners scouring every land to find some drink that will tickle [the king's] palate: an army of cooks contrives dishes for his delight."

When Alexander the Great conquered the Persian Empire seventy years later, he mocked their extravagant diet and concluded that the Persians' indulgence in culinary pleasure had weakened them and led to their downfall. Nevertheless, he stayed on at the royal city of Persepolis for several months after winning his decisive battle, celebrating the Persian New Year, adopting traditional Persian dress, and—one can only assume—enjoying plenty of Persian food. What's more, when Alexander and his army headed home to Greece, they took care to stuff their sacks with Iran's most iconic native ingredients, including pistachios, saffron, and, of course, pomegranates.

ALONG THE SILK ROAD

When taking the long view of Persian culinary history, pomegranates are an excellent place to start. In the 1930s, archaeologists unearthed a cache of over thirty thousand inscribed stone tablets at the ruins of Persepolis, the ceremonial capital of the Persian Empire from 515 to 330 BCE.

The tablets contain detailed records of government salaries paid for in food, and they reveal that the pantry staples of the earliest Iranians included walnuts, poultry, and pomegranate syrup, the key ingredients still used in the sweet-tart pomegranate stew known as *fesenjan*. Likewise, modern-day Iranian ingredients such as lamb, parsley, almonds, pistachios, vinegar, honey, onions, and garlic were already widely in use in the era of Persepolis. Incredibly, the foods that sustain and inspire Iranians today appear to be the very same ones they've been cooking with for at least twenty-five hundred years.

Although Alexander's conquest of Iran was followed many centuries later by Arab, Turk, Mongol, and Uzbek invasions, native Iranian culture and food traditions continued to flourish. One after the other, the occupiers were charmed and eventually converted to the Persian way of life. Meanwhile, Persian cuisine assimilated the best parts of these foreign culinary customs.

As the boundaries of the Persian Empire extended at various times from Egypt to India, and from Greece to Russia, this ability to embrace foreign ingredients made Persian cuisine perhaps the most sophisticated in the world. In fact, outside influences contributed to some of Iran's greatest culinary achievements.

The tomato is a good example. Following the Spanish conquest of the Americas, tomatoes reached Iran by way of the Ottoman Empire. At first, they were regarded suspiciously, as they belonged to the same family (Solanaceae) as the poison-producing deadly nightshade plant. The name for tomato in Persian, *gojeh farangi*, translates as "foreign plum," reflecting the initial wariness toward this strange red fruit. As with so many other adopted ingredients, however, tomatoes eventually became an integral part of Iranian cooking, as evidenced by such beloved dishes as *Salad Shirazi* (Tomato and Cucumber Salad, page 59), *Bademjan* (Eggplant and Tomato Stew with Pomegranate Molasses, page 107), and *Mirza Ghasemi* (Garlicky Eggplant and Tomato Spread, page 34). Other New World ingredients that blended seamlessly into the tapestry of Persian food include potatoes, winter squashes, and turkey.

FROM PERSIA TO THE WORLD

Of course, Iran's culinary influence flowed outward, as well. After the Muslim conquest of Iran in the mid-700s, the Arabs imported Persian tastes and techniques to the countries they conquered: thus, *khoresh* stew became *tagine* in Morocco; saffron *polo*, rice cooked with meat, became paella in Spain; and preserved quinces and bitter oranges reached England via trade routes from Spain and Portugal to become marmalade.

The Zoroastrians who fled to India in order to escape Muslim conversion in the ninth century (becoming the modern-day Parsis) brought their beloved *polo*, *nān* (bread), and *tanur*, which would become the pilaf, naan, and tandoori that we see on Indian menus today. Farther east, trading along the Silk Road brought Persian staples like eggplant, sesame seeds, and even garlic to China. The kebab, Iran's greatest contribution to the world catalog of handheld foods, would become a perennial American barbecue favorite starting in the late twentieth century.

Iran was not only an exporter of cooking styles, but of spiritual practices as well. In pre-Islamic Iran, the sovereign religion was Zoroastrianism, a monotheistic faith that predates Christ by six hundred years and whose narrative lent both Judaism and Christianity some of their core concepts. Familiar ideas like heaven and hell, angels, the coming of the messiah, the six days of creation, and the Ten Commandments, not to mention the date of Christmas and the ritual decoration of trees, all have antecedents in Zoroastrianism.

Many of Zoroastrianism's tenets reached Europe via Mithraism, the powerful Roman cult of the Persian sun deity, Mithra (whose birthday was December 21, the winter solstice), which was spread throughout the Roman Empire by traveling Roman legions. When the Roman emperor Constantine famously declared himself and his empire Christian in CE 313, he appropriated much of Mithraism's ritual and imagery. The link between Zoroastrianism and the Abrahamic faiths is a reminder that Europe and Asia have been exchanging ideas for millennia, and it's a clear indication of Iran's influence on Western culture.

OF MOUNTAINS AND DESERTS

The dramatic climate and geography of Iran have played a powerful role in shaping its unique cuisine. On a topographical map, the country resembles a flaring dragon's jaw that hinges in the northwest and breathes fire toward the southeast. The "jaw" is made up of two great mountain ranges: the northern Alborz Mountains, which run parallel to the Caspian Sea from Azerbaijan in the northwest all the way east to the Hindu Kush of Afghanistan; and the Zagros Mountains, which descend from the same corner in Azerbaijan all the way down the western half of the country toward the Persian Gulf in the south.

From above, Iran can be seen as a kind of massive land-bridge, slapped over the watery divide between the Middle East and the Far East. Although a great swath of north-eastern and central Iran remains uninhabitable desert, the country has a variable climate with four distinct seasons. Inside its borders, the atmospheric conditions range from permanent snow (and world-class skiing) in the Alborz Mountains to the green and rainy basin of the Caspian, from subtropical forests near the southern Gulf coast to the grassy steppes of the far north near Turkmenistan.

Divided by mountains and deserts, Iran's civilization developed in isolated pockets that weren't well connected by roads and railways until the twentieth century. These separations gave rise to contrasting cuisines in the country's diverse locales.

Each region of Iran, for instance, makes its own version of flatbread and is renowned for a unique sweet treat: chewy *gaz* nougat in Isfahan, caramelized *sohan* brittle in Qom, rose water–scented baklava in Yazd, and intricately stamped *kaloocheh* pastries in Fuman. Down on the Persian Gulf, locals concoct spicy seafood dishes that are considered too hot for the temperate tongues of their countrymen farther north.

In the northwest, the cuisine is heavily influenced by Iran's northern neighbor, Turkey, and local specialties include stuffed grape leaves, Turkish coffee, and Tabrizi meatballs filled with hard-boiled egg and prunes or apricots. The northern coastal province of Gilan is known for the country's best rice, smoked fish, and salty fish roe fresh from the Caspian Sea, as well as the tastiest *fesenjan* in the country.

A HISTORY OF HEALTHY COOKING

The common thread that connects these diverse regional styles is a shared emphasis on sweet-and-sour and fruity tastes. There is even a special word in the Persian language used to describe this distinct vinegar-and-honey quality: *malas*. Persians genuinely love tart food, and you'll see the combination of sweet and sour everywhere, from *fesenjan* stew to sour cherry preserves to dates pickled in tamarind. Acidic ingredients like rhubarb, barberries, sumac, limes, lemons, sour oranges, and vinegar all contribute to the mouth-puckering, vibrant character of Persian food.

Maybe the ancient Persians were aware of the many health benefits of sour food. Sure enough, modern studies suggest that sour juices and vinegar are antimicrobial, hydrating, and help prevent the body from storing excess fat.

Most Iranians will happily explain to you why Persian cooking is healthier than other kinds of cooking, and they're not simply boasting. Traditional Persian recipes and menus have evolved over generations based on the way the ingredients complement one another, according to a highly detailed philosophy dating back at least as far as the advent of Zoroastrianism in about 600 BCE. This system classifies all foods as either "cold" (*sarmi*) or "hot" (*gardi*). It's a system not unlike the Chinese designations of "yin" or "yang," or the Indian Ayurvedic guidelines that balance the five elements of earth, ether, air, fire, and water.

According to Persian food protocol, kebab is always sprinkled with sumac and eaten with rice, raw onion, and the yogurt drink *doogh*. Why? Well, because onions are antibacterial, and sumac and yogurt aid in digestion. This way all the ingredients conspire to help your body digest those big hunks of rich protein. In this case, the meat and onions are considered "hot," while sumac, yogurt, and rice are classified as "cold."

A PLATEFUL OF POETRY

*The feasts in the East last all the day long; they pass their time away in . . .
Reading and hearing People Read, in repeating Verses, and hearing People
Sing well, in the nature of a Chorus, the Actions of the Kings of Persia.*

—Jean Chardin, *Travels in Persia, 1673–1677*

No discussion of Persian food would be complete without a mention of Persian poetry. Mystical, often melancholy, the ageless words of poets like Hafez, Rumi, and Sa'adi are voiced in recitation and song at many Persian gatherings. Indeed, poetry and food have been called the anchors of Persian identity.

On *Shab-e Yalda*, the longest night of the year, for instance, it's customary to eat watermelon and summer fruits in the hope that the crops will thrive the following summer—and to stay up all night reading poetry. At *Norooz*, the Persian New Year which falls on the spring equinox, Iranians prepare a meal with fresh green herbs to symbolize rebirth; and even today, prominent Iranian poets pay homage to this ancient holiday by writing odes to the glory of spring. At a Persian wedding, the bride and groom feed each other honey in a ritual that invites sweetness into married life, while on the ceremonial wedding table, called a *sofreh*, one often finds a collection of Hafez along with a copy of the Koran.

FOOD FOR THOUGHT

With or without poetry, the refined and hospitable nature of Iranians is perhaps nowhere more evident than at the dinner table. If you've ever had the good fortune to be invited to a Persian home for a meal, you know that Iranians could not be less like the stereotype of angry, anti-American fanatics often portrayed in Western media. For the most part, today's Iranians are an intellectually curious, poetically inclined, and refreshingly warm people who love nothing more than to get you stuffed on delicious food, then hand you a glass of *chai* and engage you in an energetic conversation about history or philosophy.

Despite the many ways that they have elevated global cuisine, and even influenced world culture, Iranians are still a mystery to most Westerners. Still, a feast of saffron, pistachios, and pomegranates can explain more about the Iranian character than any news story, and can serve to bridge the distance between our two cultures. After twenty-five hundred years of refinement and evolution, it seems the perfect time for Persian cuisine to assume its rightful place as one of the world's great culinary traditions. *Nooshe jan!**

* "Bon appétit!"

A Guide to Persian Ingredients
A GARDEN OF EARTHLY DELIGHTS

iscovering Persian ingredients is a bit like lifting the lid off of a treasure box: the dazzling sight of pink rose petals and green cardamom is surpassed only by the heady scent and delicate flavor of red saffron and golden turmeric. In part, Persian food makes such a striking first impression because the exquisite ingredients—and the innovative way they're combined—are so entirely unique to Persian cuisine.

Following is a selection of key Persian ingredients and a brief description of how to use them. Many of these ingredients, although certainly exotic, are widely available at natural foods and gourmet markets, as well as many ethnic food stores. If you can't find these ingredients locally, you can find mail-order sources for the nonperishable goods in the Resources section (page 189).

CARAMELIZED ONIONS

Dark, sweet caramelized onions provide the foundation of flavor in many Persian stews, stuffings, rice dishes, and soups. They're especially important for giving a deep, well-rounded taste to vegetarian dishes.

How to Prepare Caramelized Onions the Persian Way

To make caramelized onions, slice the onions to a uniform thickness of $1/4$ inch or less, sauté them in oil over medium-high heat for 10 minutes, until they start to darken, then cook them slowly over low heat for about 30 minutes, until they are dark brown and roughly half their original volume. If you like, you can even caramelize a big batch of onions and store them in the refrigerator or freezer and use them as needed, or when you want to add a shot of flavor to any dish. The onions will keep in the refrigerator for up to 5 days and in an airtight container in the freezer for a couple of months.

CARDAMOM (HEL)

Originally from the south of India, cardamom, with its sweet and spicy taste, became an integral part of Persian cuisine thousands of years ago. Grassy green cardamom pods hold tiny black seeds that burst with fragrant sweetness. Iranians use cardamom in their cooking in much the way Westerners use cinnamon, and it's an element in virtually every Persian pastry and dessert. While it's easiest to use the ground cardamom available in stores (which is made from the combined pods and seeds), fastidious Persian cooks buy the pods only, break them open with a hammer or the flat side of a knife, and grind the seeds as needed. This approach makes sense given that the flavor of cardamom fades relatively quickly. Besides desserts, cardamom is also part of a classic Persian spice mix called *advieh* (comparable to an Indian garam masala mix) that can also include turmeric, saffron, black pepper, and cumin. (*See photo on page 118.*)

DATES (KHORMA)

Chewy, sugary dates are native to the Persian Gulf region. They add a note of honey to many Persian dishes, both savory and sweet, and are a prized part of the customary fruit and nut platter that Persians prepare for visiting guests. Dates have a special place at the Muslim holiday Ramadan, when the daily fast is broken at sundown by eating three dates, as the Prophet Mohammed is said to have done. There are many different date products readily available in Iran and the Middle East that aren't common in the United States, such as date paste, date molasses, and date sugar, which is made from ground and dried dates and makes a good alternative to regular sugar. The two kinds of dates most widely found in the States are soft Medjools and semidry Deglets. With their rich flavor, natural sweetness, and creamy texture, Medjools are by far the superior choice, but Deglets make an acceptable substitute. (*See photo of fresh dates on page 104.*)

DRIED LIMES (LIMOO OMANI)

Khaki-colored sun-dried limes are one of the standout ingredients of Persian cuisine, and their intense citrus essence is an iconic component of the Persian flavor profile. Dried limes are native to the Gulf state Oman (*limoo Omani* means "Omani limes"), where they are simply called *limoo*. Like regular limes, they're bitter and sweet at the same time, but have a far more intense flavor because they combine the taste of the juice and the rind. For lime and lemon lovers, they're a dream come true, yet their unmistakable taste does take some getting used to.

Dried limes are thrown whole into soups and stews. Unlike whole spices like bay leaves or cinnamon sticks that you would discard after cooking, you can cut up the softened limes and eat them—rind and all—along with the dish. The taste of a cooked dried lime is truly remarkable.

It's essential that the limes be perforated before cooking, so that the cooking liquid can be easily infused with their flavor. The limes are hard, like hollow rocks. Before cooking, soak the limes in very hot water—just enough to cover—to soften their exteriors. After fifteen minutes, you can easily pierce them with a fork or make incisions with a paring knife. You can then add the limes to whatever you're cooking. Depending on the recipe, you can add the soaking water, too, as it's full of concentrated flavor, or dilute it with water and drink it like lemonade. When cooking limes in a stew or rice dish, press on them every so often with a wooden spoon to extract their juice as the dish cooks.

Dried limes are sold both whole and ground, and the ground form is used as a seasoning similar to lime zest. (*See photo on page 162.*)

GHEE

Ghee is pure butterfat—it's melted butter with the protein and milk solids skimmed off. It is considered a healthy food in the Indian Ayurvedic tradition and can be used for cooking at temperatures up to 400°F, unlike olive and other vegetable oils, which will smoke and become toxic at high temperatures. Ghee is sold in Indian stores, or you can make it at home.

GREEN HERBS (*SABZI*)

Fresh and dried green herbs play many roles in Persian food, from colorful garnish to flavor component to main ingredient. The best example of the latter is *ghormeh sabzi* stew (Green Herb and Kidney Bean Stew, page 155), a steaming herbal gumbo colored emerald green by the volume of parsley, cilantro, scallions, and spinach that is melted down to form its thick vegetal bouquet.

The herbs most commonly used in Persian cooking are dill, mint, parsley, cilantro, basil, chives, and tarragon, while marjoram and oregano make occasional appearances. Smoky, bitter fenugreek leaves are also a major player in Persian food, but they are tricky to find in the United States, so I've left them out of the recipes. If you find fenugreek, throw several large handfuls into your *ghormeh sabzi*! For the most part, you can mix and match the herbs liberally in recipes where they're called for, swapping out cilantro for parsley or mint as needed.

It can be time-consuming to clean and chop the volume of herbs that's called for in Persian recipes, and many Persian cooks use dried herbs for just that reason. Often, dry herbs can make a fine substitute (in particular, it's frequently preferable to choose dried mint over fresh), but in many recipes, like the *ghormeh sabzi*, using fresh herbs really does result in a better-tasting dish. Fortunately, there are a few shortcuts for prepping herbs:

- Clean, dry, and chop a large volume of fresh herbs, and then freeze them. Add the frozen herbs to soup, stew, and rice recipes as needed.
- Instead of chopping by hand, pulse clean, dry herbs in a food processor.
- When using cilantro, tarragon, or dill, it's necessary to cut off the thick, fibrous ends of the stems, but there's no need to painstakingly separate every bit of stem from the leaves. In fact, all but the very ends can be used. Simply slice or mince the stems finely along with the leaves.

MINT (NA'NA)

Both full-flavored dried mint and mild fresh spearmint are used often in Persian cooking. Although in the West we usually associate mint with dessert or tea, Iranians use mint the way that Americans use cilantro or parsley.

For cooking, spearmint is the best choice. It has a more resonant, savory taste than sweet peppermint, which is primarily used to make mint tea, or generic "mint," which has a milder flavor. Look for dried spearmint in the spice aisle of gourmet and Middle Eastern food markets. At Kalustyan's in New York City (see page 189), I buy a delicious variety labeled "Egyptian spearmint." When shopping for fresh mint, look for either spearmint or the more common generic mint, a fine substitute.

Because mint is used so often in Persian cooking, and because dried mint is just as good if not better than fresh, it's helpful to keep a stock of dried mint in the pantry. To make your own dried mint, separate fresh spearmint leaves from their stems, wash them in cold water, and dry them thoroughly in a salad spinner. Turn your oven to its lowest setting and spread the herbs on baking sheets in a single layer. Dry the herbs in the oven, stirring gently every 10 minutes or so to prevent burning, until they're dry and crackly. Store the dried mint in airtight containers.

PISTACHIOS (PESTEH)

If you receive an invitation to an Iranian home, purchase good-quality roasted pistachios in the shell and take them as a gift. Your host will be delighted. While Iranians prize their dried fruit and nuts—which are often sold in upscale boutiques comparable to choco-late shops in the United States—pistachios are possibly the most beloved treat of all. Pistachios are native to Iran and are deeply intertwined with Iranian food history. Today, these nuts are cultivated in the hot desert oases of southeastern Iran. They are still used so often that they may appear many times in the course of a Persian meal.

For snacking, buy pistachios in the shell because they're the freshest, but when following a recipe that calls for pistachios, use shelled pistachios, rather than shelling them yourself. Although they may not match the quality of pistachios in the shell, it can take a long time (and many battered fingernails) to shell even a small quantity. Select the best nuts you can find, and check before buying to make sure they're not rancid. Once purchased, store pistachios in the refrigerator or freezer to preserve their freshness. (*See photo on page 38.*)

POMEGRANATES (*ANAR*)

Pomegranates are perhaps the most iconic of Iran's native foods. They are believed to have originated in Iran, and to this day more than half of the world's pomegranates are grown there. It's no wonder then that they play such a big role in Persian cuisine.

One of the most distinctive characteristics of Persian cooking is the pairing of sour fruits with savory ingredients like lamb, chicken, caramelized onions, and nuts. Pomegranates demonstrate the perfection of this pairing more than any other fruit. A good example is the northern Iranian–style Lamb Kebabs in Pomegranate-Walnut Marinade (page 95), in which pomegranate molasses gives the dish its signature sweet-and-sour taste.

If you visit Iran or its neighbor Turkey, you can enjoy a glass of freshly squeezed pomegranate juice, a tart, refreshing pick-me-up that's pressed by hand by brawny young street vendors right before your eyes. This bracing treat aside, pomegranates usually show up in Persian cuisine in one of two forms: fresh seeds or a reduction of pomegranate juice known as pomegranate molasses.

Pomegranate molasses is made from pomegranate juice that has been cooked down, and it may or may not have added sugar. These days, you can find pomegranate molasses at many gourmet and natural foods stores. Alternatively, if you can find pomegranate juice—which has become very popular in the last decade—you can make your own molasses by reducing the juice in a pan over high heat until it's thick enough to coat the back of a spoon. You may come across a product labeled "pomegranate syrup," which is much thinner and sweeter than pomegranate molasses; it's meant for use in mixed drinks as opposed to cooking and is made with artificial pomegranate flavoring as opposed to real fruit juice.

ROSE WATER AND ROSE PETALS (*GOLAB* AND *BARG-E GOL*)

Roses have been an integral part of Persian cooking and culture for thousands of years. In Sufism, the mystical branch of Islam most famous for its whirling dervishes, the rose is extolled as "the Mother of Scents and the Queen of the Garden," its "beauty and sweetness" symbolizing "the mystic path to God and enlightenment" (from *The Book of Sufi*

Healing by Shaykh Hakim Chishti). It's believed that they were first cultivated in Iran, and that the process of making rose *attar*, or "oil"—the basis of all rose perfumes—was developed there, as well. In Persian culture, the rose transcends gardens and bouquets and becomes an essential ingredient, in the form of either rose water or rose petals (usually dried).

Think of rose water as the Iranian equivalent of vanilla extract. You'll encounter its flavor in baklava, rice pudding, cookies, and ice cream. The taste of rose water can be off-putting at first—we're not used to such flowery flavors in the West—but it can really grow on you.

Rose petals lend a surprisingly savory flavor to rice, and they make a graceful garnish for yogurt and salads. When buying dried culinary roses, look for full buds, which retain their flavor better than petals. Before cooking, pull the rosebuds apart and remove the white outer petals and the remains of the stem, both of which are bitter. A good option for sourcing rose petals is your own garden. Unfortunately, virtually all store-bought roses are sprayed with pesticides, so your best bet is to dry roses that you grow yourself, without chemicals. A good culinary rose is one that has a strong, pleasing scent, no matter the color. Take a bite of a petal, and if it tastes good, you can eat the rose fresh or dried. Fresh petals can be cooked just like dried ones; in addition, you can add them to salads, lay them in sandwiches, or chop them up and stir them into honey or jam. To make aromatic rose sugar, submerge fresh (but not wet) roses in sugar and let them infuse for about a month.

SAFFRON (*ZAFARAN*)

Saffron blazes an orange trail across the whole of Persian cuisine, flavoring entrées, desserts, and rice with its unmistakable scent. Long used as a medicine and a perfume, saffron is almost certainly the world's sexiest spice. In the dialogue of seduction known as the Song of Solomon, from the Old Testament, the man compares his lover to a fertile garden, full of fragrant plants like "spikenard and saffron."

Saffron is believed to have originated on the island of Crete. The Persians carried it east around 500 BCE, and today Iran is the world's biggest producer of the spice. Iranian saffron is considered the world's best, and if you're lucky enough to obtain a thin plastic disk of it etched in gold Persian lettering, you will have enough to make several excellent batches of saffron-scented rice, stew, or pastry.

Saffron is infamous for its high price, worth more than gold by weight, because it is painstakingly harvested by gently plucking the stigma from the center of the fall-flowering purple crocus. Fortunately, a little goes a long way. It takes only a teaspoon or less to flavor a whole dish—more than that and it can take on a metallic, bitter taste. When purchasing saffron, always buy the full strands rather than the ground spice; that way you're assured of getting real saffron and not a cheap imitation or a mixture diluted with other spices—a common scam throughout the ages that continues to this day. (*See photo on page 68.*)

How to Prepare Saffron for Cooking the Persian Way

When using saffron in a recipe, first measure out the amount that's called for. Then, using a mortar and pestle, grind the strands to release their volatile oils and draw out their flavor. Iranians typically grind saffron in a small mortar made out of brass, but the more common ceramic or stone variety works just as well.

If your saffron is even a little moist, it can be hard to grind. To make sure it's dry, heat your oven to its lowest setting, spread the saffron on a clean, dry baking sheet, and put it in the oven for about 5 minutes. Let it cool, then transfer the saffron to the mortar. Add a pinch of sugar or salt, which makes grinding easier, and grind the saffron into a powder.

Now, transfer the saffron to a small bowl. Bring some water or stock to a boil and let it cool for a few minutes. Alternatively, you can heat milk, butter, or oil. Pour hot liquid equal to two to three times the amount of saffron into the bowl. The hot liquid helps to both activate the flavor and intensify the color of the saffron. Gently swirl the saffron with the liquid, and let it steep until you're ready to use. When the recipe calls for adding the saffron, add the entire contents of the bowl.

The process of preparing saffron with a mortar and pestle takes a few minutes and requires a special piece of equipment, but there is something magical about grinding the spice using the same method that's been used for thousands of years, and it's a good way to adjust your mindset to the ancient traditions in which Persian cooking is rooted.

To save time, take a tip from Persian cooks who use the spice on a daily basis: grind up a large batch of saffron, steep it in liquid, then cool and store it in the refrigerator in a sealed jar for the next several weeks, using a teaspoon or two of the liquid in recipes as needed. You can also use a clean electric spice grinder to grind the saffron, which works most effectively if you grind at least a tablespoon at a time, along with the equivalent of a cube of sugar.

SUMAC (*SOMAGH*)

Purplish-red sumac is a tart, coarse powder made from the red berries of the sumac shrub. Seasoning food with sumac has a similar effect to seasoning with lemon juice, but sumac has a milder, brinier taste because of the salt that's added to facilitate the grinding process. You may have tasted sumac before in *za'atar*, the Arabic spice mixture that combines sumac with thyme and sesame seeds. In Persian cooking, sumac is used to season the saffron rice that accompanies kebabs. You'll find it on the table at a Persian restaurant as surely as you will see salt and pepper in an American establishment. The fruity sourness of sumac complements fish, chicken, and vegetables equally well.

The edible staghorn variety of sumac grows wild in the United States and has a place in Native American cookery. In fact, a traditional Native American drink is "sumac-ade," made by submerging the berries in water and rubbing and crushing them to extract their flavor. Strained sumac-ade is high in vitamin C and can be sweetened and enjoyed just like lemonade. On their own, fresh sumac berries make a tart, chewy trail snack.

Look for wild sumac on roadsides and in open woods and clearings. In the late autumn, you'll see the plants bursting with bright red cone-shaped clusters of seedless berries. Dry the berries and grind them up with a little salt to make your own stash of sumac powder. If you're concerned about encountering poison sumac by mistake, don't be; it's almost exclusively limited to swamps, and luckily, the two plants look very different. Poison sumac has white, hanging berries and short, smooth leaves, as opposed to staghorn sumac's red berries and jagged leaves. (*See photo on page 82.*)

TAMARIND (*TAMBREHIND*)

When tempered with sugar, tart tamarind fruit transforms into a deliciously tangy condiment. Although native to Africa, tamarind has been a key ingredient in Southeast Asian cooking for thousands of years, where you'll find it in chutney, *pad Thai*, and various curries. It's believed that the word "tamarind" comes from the Persian *tamar-i-hindi*, or "Indian date," so named because the pulp looks similar to a date.

Tamarind and seafood have a special affinity and it's common to find them paired in recipes like the spicy *Ghaliyeh Mahi* (Persian Gulf–Style Spicy Tamarind Fish Stew, page 117). Not surprisingly, tamarind is most often used in southern Iran, near the Persian Gulf, the part of the country closest to both Africa and India, and where there is an abundance of fresh seafood.

In Western markets you'll usually find tamarind in the form of semidried pulp that needs to be soaked in hot water, worked with your hands to separate the flesh from the seeds and fiber, and pushed through a sieve.

To avoid the hassle of soaking, look for tamarind concentrate from Thailand labeled "Thai fruit" or "pure fresh tamarind concentrate." Thai tamarind concentrate, a puree with a texture similar to applesauce, is made of tamarind and water; you can easily pass it through a sieve to remove bits of seed. Its light caramel color and clean taste make it a good counterpoint to other ingredients. Find Thai tamarind concentrate at Asian food stores or online at Grocery Thai and Kalustyan's (see Resources, page 189). If you can't find Thai tamarind concentrate, a prepared tamarind chutney cooked with spices and sugar makes an acceptable substitute.

TURMERIC (*ZARDCHUBEH*)

Ground turmeric is used in virtually every Persian stew, and the mustard color that it gives to food is a memorable feature of Persian cuisine. Turmeric is a rhizome, like ginger, and its papery skin conceals bright yellow-gold flesh. It is native to India, a nearby neighbor of Iran, and is responsible for the signature yellow color of curry powder.

In Persian cooking, ground dried turmeric is used in small quantities, usually no more than a teaspoon per recipe, because it has an earthy, bitter aftertaste. When cooked down slowly, however, it adds a warm background note that subtly enhances the overall taste of a dish. Just a small amount is enough to color an entire dish. Be careful when handling turmeric, as it can stain hands and surfaces. Try using a small spoon to scoop the turmeric directly into the cooking pot, avoiding contact with your fingers.

In recent years, turmeric has been the focus of several studies documenting its potential to heal a range of ailments without causing side effects. Curcumin, the active component in turmeric, is an antioxidant, which means that it fights the free radical cells that are associated with cancer. Turmeric helps to make food more digestible because of its anti-inflammatory properties, and it has even been linked to the prevention of Alzheimer's disease. It's entirely likely that the ancient Iranians and their turmeric-loving neighbors in India understood the health benefits of this powerful spice.

YOGURT (*MAAST*)

It's rare to eat a Persian lunch or dinner without yogurt—it's simply a fixture at the Persian table. (The only exception may be at a kosher meal, where dairy and meat can't be eaten together.) Yogurt has its origins in Central Asia, and Iranians have been consuming it for literally thousands of years. Although you can purchase commercially made yogurt in Iran, many Persians there and abroad still prefer to make it at home. The now-popular thick yogurt that Americans call Greek style is everyday yogurt in Iran.

Like lemon juice, sumac, barberries, tamarind, and green plums, yogurt is yet another souring agent in the endless Persian quest for pucker-worthy substances. Yogurt makes a cool and creamy contrast to rich stews and meats, but like so many other Persian ingredients, it's a vehicle for health and is widely understood to promote healthy stomach flora through the beneficial acidophilus bacteria it contains. Iranians have found myriad ways to cook with yogurt.

A MODERN, HEALTHY SPIN ON TRADITIONAL PERSIAN RECIPES

Although the goal of this book is to shed light on Persian food, I also want to show you a sustainable approach to cooking that's good for both your body and the environment. For that reason, I've kept fried food and red meat to a minimum, and I've highlighted all of the vibrant seasonal ingredients that make this cuisine unique. In order to make these delectable dishes more nourishing, there are a few key areas where I've modified the recipes from what you might find in a standard Persian cookbook. In particular, you'll find healthy alternatives in the areas of cooking oil, sweeteners, and grains.

Cooking Oils

Olive oil is still the tastiest oil that I know of, and it's certainly one of the most healthy. However, extra-virgin olive oil is not considered viable for high-heat cooking, as it has a low smoke point of 375°F. I mostly save extra-virgin olive oil for marinades, low-heat cooking, and for drizzling onto food as a garnish just before serving. If you're very partial to olive oil, you'll find that extra-light olive oil, with a smoke point of around 468°F, is suitable for frying and other high-temperature applications. My number one choice in these recipes, however, is grapeseed oil, a pleasantly neutral-tasting, all-purpose oil with a similarly high smoke point; it also doubles as a reliable option for vinaigrettes. The fats and oils listed below are excellent alternatives to explore.

Oils for high-heat cooking

Almond oil • avocado oil • extra-light or refined olive oil • ghee or clarified butter • grapeseed oil • refined coconut oil* • refined peanut oil • refined sesame oil • rice bran oil • sunflower oil

*Note: This is *not* the same thing as "partially hydrogenated coconut oil," which was widely criticized in the 1990s for its unusually high level of saturated fat.

Oils for sautéing

Ghee • grapeseed oil • organic canola oil • peanut oil • refined sesame oil • safflower oil • sunflower oil • unrefined, cold-pressed, and expeller-pressed coconut oil

Oils for garnishing, flavoring, and finishing

Extra-virgin olive oil • toasted sesame oil • unrefined nut and seed oils, such as pumpkin seed, walnut, hazelnut, hemp, and flaxseed

Sweeteners

I recommend avoiding white sugar if possible. The reasons are simple and hardly controversial: it's bad for your health, as well as harmful for the environment and questionable in terms of human rights. In terms of how they affect your body, natural sweeteners like the ones below aren't so different from white sugar, but they have more nutrients and do not entail the same chemical processes and environmental hazards. I believe that sugar has a place in our diet when used in moderation, and it's good to be aware of how much of it you consume, both for your health and to keep the enjoyment of sweets a special and celebratory experience.

For most of the recipes in this book, my sweetener of choice is organic cane sugar, a light beige sugar that's slightly less processed than regular white cane sugar and is widely available in natural food stores (plain white sugar can be swapped out for organic cane sugar with little difference in the final result). However, all of the sweeteners on the list below are good ones to experiment with. If a recipe calls for organic cane sugar, you can substitute one of the dry sweeteners; and if a recipe calls for honey, you can use any one of the liquid sweeteners. Experimenting with these ingredients means you will have varying tastes, colors, and textures in your dishes, but trying them out is the best way to learn about their subtleties and sweetness levels. Look for these sweeteners at natural foods stores or at online retailers (see page 189).

Dry sweeteners

Coconut sugar • date sugar • evaporated cane juice • jaggery • maple sugar • muscovado sugar • organic cane sugar • stevia • unrefined brown sugar

Liquid sweeteners

Apple syrup, aka *appelstroop* • brown rice syrup • fruit juices, such as pear, peach, apricot, apple, white grape, and orange • honey • maple syrup

Grains and Flours

As much as possible, I've tried to integrate unrefined whole grains and traditional Middle Eastern flours into these recipes. I've done this partly because of the lack of nutrition in white flour and processed grains, and of our growing awareness about gluten intolerance. Mainly though, I love the interesting tastes and textures of grains such as millet, quinoa, and brown rice, along with flours made from foods like coconut, chickpeas, fava beans, and tapioca. These whole grains and grain flours can be found at natural foods stores and online (see page 189). If a recipe calls for whole-grain flour, you can always use regular white flour in its place.

Iranians use white rice to create all kinds of spectacular rice dishes. Although white rice is easy to prepare and has a sweet, pleasing taste, it can be unhealthy if eaten on a regular basis. White rice is a processed grain that has had the bran and germ stripped out, so it has a low nutrient content. White rice hits the bloodstream a lot like white sugar, and there's new research that links eating white rice to type 2 diabetes. Fortunately, you can cook any of the rice dishes in this book using quinoa, brown rice, millet, or other whole grains.

Whole grains to substitute for white basmati rice
....

Barley, pearled • brown rice • freekeh • millet • quinoa • spelt berries • steel-cut oats • wheat berries

Whole-grain and gluten-free flours
....

Barley flour • chickpea or garbanzo flour • coconut flour • fava bean flour • rice flour • spelt flour • tapioca flour

Tips for Cooking Whole Grains

Here are some tips for cooking whole grains that are fluffy and separated, and full of good flavor.

Soak 'em. Soaking grains before cooking makes them more digestible and mellows the naturally bitter taste of some grains. Grains actually taste and smell sweeter after soaking—anywhere from an hour to overnight is fine. After soaking, drain and rinse the grains under cold water. If you soak the grains for more than 4 hours, they will cook more quickly and with less water. For grains that have been soaked for more than 4 hours, use $^1/_2$ cup less water than is called for, and check for doneness after 20 minutes.

Start with boiling water. Starting with boiling water results in a fluffier grain. Always bring the water to a boil first, then add the grain to the water, or pour the water into the grain. Once the grain and water are combined, return the water to a boil, then lower the heat to a simmer and cook, covered, for the specified amount of time.

Add stock. Want more flavor in your grains? Use vegetable or chicken stock instead of water. You can also enhance the flavor of a grain by substituting a cup of tomato juice for a cup of the cooking water.

Sauté in fat. Cooking the grains in a little fat gives them more flavor and helps to ensure that they will be fluffy and separated. After soaking and rinsing the grains under cold water, add them to a dry pot over low heat and stir often until they are dry and start to give off a savory, nutty smell. When all of the soaking liquid has evaporated, add a tablespoon or two of cooking oil, and toss to coat the grains. Now, pour in the boiling water.

Let the grains rest. After the grains are cooked, turn off the heat and let them rest, covered, for about 10 minutes. This gives them time to solidify as they cool. If you dig into the grains right after cooking, they'll still be very soft, and you're likely to break them and make the texture mushy. After 10 minutes, remove the lid and fluff the grains with a fork. Now you're ready to season and serve, or continue with the rest of the recipe.

The recipes in this book were all tested with fine-grain sea salt, unless otherwise specified (as in the pickle recipes). Sea salt is made by evaporating seawater, which allows trace minerals to remain and gives the salt a mild flavor. Sea salt does not, however, contain substantial amounts of the essential nutrient iodine. Table salt, which is mined from underground salt mines, has the minerals removed and often contains added iodine, as well as an additive to prevent clumping. There's no proof that one is healthier than the other, but I think sea salt has a better, more subtle taste.

Feel free to use any salt you have on hand to make these recipes, but be aware that table salt has a sharper taste and a higher concentration of sodium than sea salt. If using a salt other than fine sea salt, I recommend using less salt than is called for in a given recipe, and instead seasoning to taste as you cook.

starters and snacks

Although you'll see them listed on Persian restaurant menus, there is really no such thing as an appetizer in Persian cooking. When you visit someone's home for lunch or dinner, you'll find bowls of fresh and dried nuts and fruit, as well as small vegetables like baby cucumbers and cherry tomatoes for snacking. There may be a plate of cookies and sweets, too. Still, you'll have no problem knowing when mealtime proper has begun, as all of the real food— the stews and rice, salads, and yogurt—will come out all at once.

There's a method to this madness. From the Persian perspective, you absolutely need the full, combined effect of the tangy yogurt dips, crunchy herbs, refreshing salads, sour pickles, and pliant, toasty breads, all working together to create a symphony of flavor. Stew without pickles, yogurt, and rice? Forget it! Like the sampling of many different tastes on an Indian *thali* plate, or the Korean spread of side dishes known as *banchan*, the point is that everything is meant to be tasted *together*. What's more, the resulting spread turns the Persian table into a gorgeous collage of colors, textures, and shapes.

Most of the dishes in this chapter can be prepared ahead of time, and they'll taste even better after sitting for a few hours or a day. This makes it easy to prepare several of them for a single meal. In fact, a liberal sampling of these light dishes will make a satisfying lunch or dinner by itself, with no real need for a main course. Try starting with a platter of *sabzi khordan*, the assortment of fresh herbs, cheese, and bread described in this chapter (page 27). Build from there with one of the brightly colored spreads, like the fuchsia Yogurt with Beets (page 35), the red Turkish Roasted Tomato and Red Pepper Dip (page 33), or the yellow-orange Garlicky Eggplant and Tomato Spread (page 34).

All of these, as well as the Yogurt with Shallots (page 36), can be enjoyed like more familiar Middle Eastern dips such as baba ghanoush and hummus, or they can serve as condiments for other foods.

Welcome to the new Persian kitchen; let's dig in!

whole grilled fava beans

Favas are especially rich and creamy beans, and Persians use them often. Peeling fresh favas is tedious, though, which is why I love this straightforward method of cooking and eating the entire bean, pod and all. This is a very casual (read "messy") dish that is best made in spring when favas first appear and are still small and tender. If you miss the first of the favas, don't worry, as you can still grill favas that are bigger and more mature later in the season; you just won't be able to eat the fibrous pods. In that case, rake the pods with your teeth to pull out the beans, like you would with edamame, and you'll still get the full garlicky flavor of the marinade.

serves 4

1 pound small, tender fava beans
   in the pod
2 cloves garlic, finely minced
1 tablespoon dried thyme, or
   2 tablespoons fresh thyme

$^1/_4$ cup grapeseed oil
3 tablespoons balsamic vinegar
1 tablespoon sea salt
Freshly ground black pepper

To remove the strings on either side of the fava bean, cut off the stem with a paring knife and pull it gently down one side of the pod; most of the thick string should come off. Do the same on the other side.

In a large bowl, whisk together the garlic, thyme, oil, and vinegar. Add the favas, season with the salt and pepper, and toss well to coat.

Prepare a hot grill.

Place the favas on the grill in a single layer in batches, if necessary. Grill for 8 to 10 minutes, basting often with the marinade. The pods will char and become soft. Turn them over and cook on the second side for 6 to 8 minutes. Test a pod to see if it's chewy and if the beans inside are tender. Transfer to a plate and serve warm.

fresh herb platter

sabzi khordan

A plate of fresh herbs is served at most Persian meals, often taking the place of a salad. Serve this dish as an appetizer, or do as the Persians do and leave it on the table throughout the meal. Toasted spices and olive oil poured over the cheese add a warming boost of flavor.

serves 4 to 6

8 ounces feta cheese
1 tablespoon coriander seeds
1 tablespoon cumin seeds
1 tablespoon caraway seeds
1/3 cup extra-virgin olive oil
Coarse salt, such as Maldon salt, fleur de sel, or kosher salt

2 bunches whole fresh herbs, in any combination: spearmint, basil, cilantro, flat-leaf parsley, tarragon, dill, chives, marjoram
1 bunch scallions, quartered crosswise, roots removed

2 cups walnuts (see Note below)
6 radishes, trimmed and quartered
Lavash or other flatbread

Drain the feta and place it in a medium bowl. Grind the spices coarsely, if desired. Heat a small skillet over high heat. Add the coriander, cumin, and caraway seeds, and shake the pan continuously until the spices start to release their aroma, about 2 minutes. Immediately transfer to a bowl and pour in the olive oil. Add a pinch of coarse salt. Swirl the spices in the oil and steep for a few minutes. Pour the mixture over the feta. You can even work it in with your hands, gently crumbling the feta, if desired.

Wash and dry the herbs. Trim the stems, but leave them intact. Place the herbs on a large platter in a few fluffy piles. Place the walnuts on the platter, along with the radishes and lavash. Transfer the feta to the platter and garnish it with coarse salt.

For a single serving, pick up a few stalks of herbs. Tear the flatbread into a manageable piece and stuff it with the herbs, walnuts, a small piece of cheese, and a radish or two. Fold and eat like a sandwich.

Note: To remove bitterness from the walnuts, place them in a bowl, add boiling water to cover and a pinch of salt, and soak from 1 hour up to overnight. Before serving, drain and rinse until the water runs clear.

winter squash fritters with rose petals

Use any winter squash in these fritters: Red Kuri, kabocha, pumpkin, and butternut are just some of the colorful varieties of these versatile vegetables that bumble into markets on wobbly bottoms at the onset of autumn. The recipe calls for chickpea flour, a traditional Persian ingredient that's available at most natural foods stores, but any flour will do. The batter can be made a day ahead and stored in the refrigerator. A few extra rose petals make a fetching garnish.

makes about 16 fritters

$^1/_2$ cup walnuts

2 tablespoons dried rose petals or dried whole rosebuds pulled apart and stems removed

6 scallions, green and white parts, coarsely chopped

2 cups peeled and grated winter squash

2 eggs, beaten

$^1/_2$ cup chickpea flour

1 teaspoon ground cumin

Sea salt

1 cup crumbled feta cheese

Ghee or other recommended oil for high heat cooking (see page 18)

Freshly ground black pepper

$^1/_2$ cup thick Greek-style yogurt

Preheat the oven to 250°F. Line a baking sheet with parchment paper.

Pulse the walnuts, rose petals, and scallions in a food processor until coarsely ground. Transfer to a large bowl and combine with the squash, eggs, flour, cumin, and 1 teaspoon salt. Mix well and fold in the feta.

Heat a skillet over medium-high heat and add ghee to coat the bottom. Drop in heaping tablespoonfuls of the batter, spacing them 1 inch apart. Cook, turning once, for about 3 minutes per side, until the fritters form a golden crust. You may need to lower the heat slightly as you cook. Drain the fritters on paper towels, then transfer to the prepared baking sheet and keep them warm in the oven until ready to serve.

Season the fritters with salt and pepper and top each with a dollop of yogurt.

new potatoes with dill and lemon

I first tasted these verdant potatoes in a Russian spa and was reminded of both the Jewish and Persian foods I grew up enjoying. No wonder, as dill is native to southern Russia and Central Asia, and both Russians and Iranians scatter this pungent herb liberally into cooked and raw foods. Dill's lively, aniselike flavor complements potatoes perfectly. If you can't find new potatoes, simply use a good waxy variety like fingerlings or red potatoes, and adjust the cooking time accordingly.

serves 6

2 pounds small new potatoes, scrubbed
$^1/_4$ cup extra-virgin olive oil
1 teaspoon grated lemon zest

$^1/_4$ cup freshly squeezed lemon juice
2 cups loosely packed fresh dill, minced

2 cloves garlic, minced
$^1/_4$ teaspoon ground turmeric
Sea salt and freshly ground black pepper

Bring a pot of generously salted water to a boil. Add the potatoes and boil for about 10 minutes, until fork-tender. Drain and let cool slightly. As soon as the potatoes are cool enough to handle, cut them in half.

While the potatoes cook, whisk together the oil, lemon zest and juice, dill, garlic, and turmeric in a large bowl. Toss the still-hot potatoes in the dressing and season with salt and pepper. Serve warm.

persian-style grilled corn

balal

Grilled corn is a popular warm-weather street food in Iran, and during corn season, vendors are out in force turning corn over hot coals until it's smoky and charred. The corn then gets a quick wash in a bath of briny water, and is then handed steaming hot to eager customers. This traditional method of preparing corn works equally well on a gas grill or over coals. The corn requires no oil or butter. Its flavor is due solely to the saltwater, the smokiness of the grill, and its own natural sweetness.

serves 4

Sea salt
4 ears corn, shucked
(leave stems on)

Prepare a hot grill.

As the grill heats, select a stockpot big enough to hold all of the corn. Fill the pot three-quarters full of water and bring it to a boil. Add enough salt to make the water very briny, about 2 tablespoons. Turn off the heat and set aside, covered.

Place the corn directly on the hot grill. Using tongs, rotate the corn once every minute or so. Grill the corn for about 10 minutes, until tender. It should be browned and charred all over, but not burned.

Immediately submerge the corn in the salty water, and swish it around with tongs to remove any charred bits or flakes. Pull out the corn and serve hot.

"Persian" or "Iranian"?

Have you ever heard of an "Iranian" restaurant? My guess is you haven't. Restaurants in America that serve food from Iran are usually called "Persian," or, even more enigmatically, "Middle Eastern," even "Mediterranean." You can't blame the restaurant owners: Due to the United States' long-running cold war with Iran, the name continues to carry negative connotations. But the debate over whether to say Persia or Iran goes back much further than the present era.

What's in a Name?

Records dating back to the Sassanid Persian Empire in the third century CE refer to a race of people known as Aryans, the root of the modern word "Iranians." Although "Aryan" is a loaded term for us today, perhaps best known for its perverse use by Nazi Germany, "Aryan" is simply a Sanskrit word meaning "noble" that was used to refer to an Indo-European people who inhabited Iran, Afghanistan, and India.

The Greeks, those famously fluent chroniclers of ancient history, called the Iranians Parsis, because the first great ruler of the Persian Empire, Cyrus the Great, was based in the province of Pars. Because our historical perspective of the ancient world was handed down to us by the Greeks, the term "Persian" has been used in the West to refer to Iranians ever since.

So, which is the correct word: "Persian" or "Iranian"? Technically, "Iranian" is the proper term. It's what people inside Iran have been calling themselves since the beginning of their history, and in practical terms, there is no place on the map called Persia. At the same time, most of the historical accomplishments of the Iranian people known to the West have been attributed to Persians, and that's how we've come to appreciate Persian poetry, astronomy, miniature painting, rug weaving—and, of course, fine Persian cuisine. I use both words interchangeably throughout the book; that way we keep ourselves grounded in reality, but we still have a little room left to dream, too.

Clockwise from left: **Yogurt with Beets** (page 35),
Turkish Roasted Tomato and Red Pepper Dip (opposite),
Garlicky Eggplant and Tomato Spread (page 34)

turkish roasted tomato and red pepper dip

The northwestern tip of Iran borders Turkey's eastern provinces, and there's a long history of shared cooking customs between the two countries. This umami-rich dip known as ezme, which tips its hat to the Persian palate, is ubiquitous in Istanbul restaurants, and ranges from the sublime to the so-so. Indeed, you'll find that the quality of the ezme is a good indicator of the quality of the food overall. When made with care, this simple spread really sings and enlivens the taste of any Mediterranean meal. It's best enjoyed within a day of being made.

makes 2 cups

3 medium to large tomatoes
(1¹/₂ pounds), halved
1 red bell pepper, halved and
seeded
1 tablespoon grapeseed oil
Sea salt and freshly ground black
pepper

2 cloves garlic, minced
1 shallot, minced
3 tablespoons extra-virgin
olive oil
1 tablespoon pomegranate
molasses

1 teaspoon smoked paprika
1 cup loosely packed fresh
flat-leaf parsley

Preheat the oven to 400°F.

Combine the tomatoes and red pepper in a large bowl and drizzle with the grapeseed oil. Season with salt and pepper, and toss well to coat. Spread the vegetables on a baking sheet, and roast, stirring occasionally, for 45 minutes, until tender. Let cool.

In a small bowl, whisk the garlic and shallot with the extra-virgin olive oil, pomegranate molasses, paprika, and a pinch of salt.

Combine the roasted vegetables, parsley, and marinade in a food processor and pulse several times until mostly smooth. Season to taste with salt and pepper, and serve.

garlicky eggplant and tomato spread

mirza ghasemi

I don't know who "Mr." or Mirza Ghasemi was, but like the anonymous father of baba ghanoush (which means "pampered daddy" in Arabic), his name lives on as a richly flavored eggplant dip that's made to be slathered on flatbread. This ocher-hued spread is thickened with scrambled eggs, which make it substantial enough to be spooned over grains for a light, satisfying meal. I advise making it a day ahead so the flavors can ripen. If you can't be bothered to skin the tomatoes, simply use a 16-ounce can of crushed tomatoes. (See photo on page 32.)

serves 4 to 6

---

1 large eggplant (1 pound), sliced
   in half lengthwise
3 medium to large tomatoes
   (1¹/₂ pounds)
3 tablespoons grapeseed oil

6 cloves garlic, minced
2 tablespoons tomato paste
¹/₂ teaspoon ground turmeric
2 eggs
3 tablespoons freshly squeezed
   lemon juice

Sea salt and freshly ground black
   pepper
1 to 2 tablespoons extra-virgin
   olive oil

Preheat the oven to 350°F. Grease a baking sheet with grapeseed oil.

Lay the eggplant face down on the baking sheet, score the skin with a fork, and bake for about 1 hour, until very tender. When cool, scoop out the flesh and coarsely chop.

Bring a small pot of water to a boil and prepare a bowl of ice water. Cut a shallow X at the base of each tomato and boil for 1 minute, then plunge in the ice water. Pull off the skin and dice small.

Heat the grapeseed oil in a large, deep skillet over medium heat and add the tomatoes, eggplant, garlic, tomato paste, and turmeric. Cook for 10 minutes, until the tomatoes are softened and the flavors of the garlic and turmeric have mellowed.

Take about ¹/₄ cup of the vegetables and whisk them with the eggs in a bowl. Add the mixture to the pan and cook, stirring occasionally, for 5 minutes, until the eggs are fully cooked. Turn off the heat and add the lemon juice. Season with salt and pepper and transfer to a serving bowl. Serve warm topped with the extra-virgin olive oil.

yogurt with beets

borani chogondar

This luminous fuchsia yogurt is traditionally made with cooked beets, but we'll save a step: the raw beets called for here will soften and mellow in the acid of the yogurt, especially if allowed to marinate for an hour before serving. A grater attachment on your food processor will make this recipe even easier, and will save your hands from staining. The natural oils in your skin will awaken the flavor of the dried mint, so rub it between your palms as you add it to the yogurt. (See photo on page 32.)

serves 6

1/2 clove garlic, minced
1 tablespoon plus 1 teaspoon
   dried mint
3 tablespoons extra-virgin
   olive oil

1 small red beet, peeled and
   grated (about 1 cup)
Sea salt
2 cups thick Greek-style yogurt
Freshly ground black pepper

In a bowl, combine the garlic, 1 tablespoon of the mint, 2 tablespoons of the olive oil, the beets, and 1 teaspoon salt. Set aside to marinate for 5 minutes.

Fold in the yogurt and season with salt and pepper. Cover and let rest for at least 1 hour, or up to 24 hours, in the refrigerator. Transfer to a serving bowl. Spoon the remaining 1 tablespoon oil over the yogurt and scatter the remaining 1 teaspoon mint over the top, and serve.

yogurt with shallots

mast-o musir

If you've ever gone to town on a bowl of sour cream and onion dip, this easy-to-make condiment will taste deliciously familiar, but without the additives and extra fat typical of store-bought dips. Serve mast-o musir *alongside rice to accompany any of the entrées in the book; its versatility complements all kinds of Persian flavors. The dip is infinitely tastier after the yogurt has had time to soften the bitter edge of the shallots, so let it mellow in the refrigerator overnight before serving.*

makes 2 cups

2 cups thick Greek-style yogurt
1 small shallot, finely minced

Sea salt and freshly ground black
 pepper

Combine the yogurt and shallot in a bowl and season with salt and pepper. Cover and refrigerate for up to 24 hours before serving.

"problem solver" nut mix

ajil-e moshkel-gosha

Both making and eating this Silk Road–style trail mix is believed to solve problems and unlock difficulties, and it's a tradition to present parcels of it to friends and even strangers at Norooz (Persian New Year) and other holidays. I first tasted this sweet-and-salty treat at my cousin Mahin's house.

Mahin's version, below, features distinctly Persian ingredients like dried mulberries, roasted chickpeas, and pistachios, which you can find at the markets and online stores listed in the Resources section (page 189). But the possibilities are endless; try pumpkin seeds, peanuts, walnuts, popcorn, dates, dried apricots, cherries, goji berries, shaved coconut, or dark chocolate chips, and watch as your problems resolve themselves!

makes 2 cups

$^1/_2$ cup green raisins
$^1/_4$ cup dried mulberries
$^1/_4$ cup roasted chickpeas

$^1/_4$ cup toasted almonds
$^1/_4$ cup toasted hazelnuts

$^1/_4$ cup toasted cashews
$^1/_4$ cup pistachios

Combine all of the ingredients and store in an airtight container for up to 1 month.

passover charoset

Charoset, a compote of nuts, fruit, and honey, is typically eaten during Passover. Its dense, syrupy texture is meant to evoke the mortar that Jews labored with when they were enslaved in Egypt. At the Passover Seder, charoset is often paired with the ritual bitter herb, horse-radish, and eaten on matzoh in what's known as a Hillel sandwich, a heavenly fusion of salt and sweet.

makes about 4 cups

8 Medjool dates, pitted and finely chopped
2 tablespoons honey
2 tablespoons pomegranate molasses

$^1/_4$ teaspoon ground cardamom
$^1/_4$ teaspoon ground cinnamon
$^1/_4$ teaspoon sea salt
2 crisp, sweet apples, such as Fuji, finely diced

$^3/_4$ cup toasted walnuts
$^3/_4$ cup toasted almonds
$^1/_4$ cup toasted pistachios

In a large bowl, whisk together the dates, honey, pomegranate molasses, cardamom, cinnamon, and salt. Add the apples and toss to coat. Pulse the walnuts, almonds, and pistachios in a food processor about 10 times, until very coarsely ground, and combine them with the apples. The charoset can be made a day ahead and stored in the refrigerator.

soups

One frosty February Sunday last year, I went to visit my friend Somayeh in her tiny grad student walk-up in West Philly. Over the course of the afternoon, I watched with awe as she produced an elaborate feast of stew, rice with *tahdig* (see page 128), herbed yogurt, and salad from her Lilliputian kitchen. In the last hour of cooking, she whipped up a humble Oatmeal and Mushroom Soup (page 50) seasoned with turmeric, lime juice, and cream. It was important to her that she make me a proper and complete Persian meal, so leaving out the soup wasn't an option. Of all the delicious foods she cooked that day, the memory of the gentle, velvety soup that finally restored warmth to my fingertips is what has lingered the longest.

The role of soup in Persian food can't be overstated; indeed, the very word for "cook" is *ash-paz*, literally "soup maker," and "kitchen" translates as *ash-paz khaneh*, or "the soup maker's room." More than a mere course, soup in the Persian kitchen is a symbolic dish that transmits a message—a culinary prayer, if you will—whose ingredients and fragrances form a kind of gastronomic language that's been spoken by Persians for millennia.

For example, there's "charity soup." In this tradition, each neighborhood family contributes ingredients and helps prepare the soup according to its means, and then distributes the dish to the entire community, both rich and poor. A "pledge soup," meanwhile, is made in hopes of healing the sick or bringing a lost family member back home. If the prayer is answered, the cook pledges to make the soup on every anniversary of the happy occasion. During the *Norooz* (Persian New Year) holiday, and whenever a loved one leaves for a long journey, it's customary to prepare the noodle soup *ash-e reshteh* (Bean, Herb, and Noodle Soup, page 53); the long strands of noodles symbolize the winding path of life.

Typically, Persian soups are not light and brothy, but thick with beans, herbs, and grains. Like the Asian rice porridge congee, these hearty soups can be enjoyed at breakfast, or served as a meal on their own at lunch or dinner. Some of the soups in this chapter are quite traditional—like the Cold Pistachio Soup with Mint and Leeks (opposite), Pomegranate Soup (page 48), and Persian "Matzoh Balls" with Chickpeas and Chicken (page 47)—while others, like the Saffron Corn Soup (page 43) and Cleansing Spring Nettle Soup (page 52), are original creations that pay homage to the time-honored Persian soup tradition.

cold pistachio soup with mint and leeks

soup-e pesteh

This silky soup is something of a Persian vichyssoise, the storied cold potato potage with the French name. Westerners have long perceived French culture as the height of refinement, and Iranians are no different. Quite a few French words have entered the common Persian parlance, such as merci *(thanks),* valise *(suitcase), and even* gourmet. *(Ironically, vichyssoise was actually invented in America!) Surprisingly rich for a dairy-free dish, this soup can be served warm just after blending, or sipped cold as a refreshing summer starter. The green leek tops give it its bright, grassy color.*

serves 4 to 6

3 tablespoons grapeseed oil
1 pound leeks, green and white
    parts, coarsely chopped
1 cup pistachios
1 clove garlic, minced

$^1/_2$ teaspoon ground cumin
Sea salt
7 cups chicken stock, vegetable
    stock, or water

About 2 cups loosely packed
    fresh spearmint
Juice of 2 lemons
Freshly ground black pepper

Heat the oil in a large, deep skillet over medium-high heat. Add the leeks and cook, stirring occasionally, about 10 minutes, until soft. Cook the leeks in batches, if they don't all fit at once.

Stir in the pistachios, garlic, cumin, and 1 teaspoon salt, and cook for 1 minute. Add the stock and bring to a boil; then lower the heat and simmer, uncovered, for 10 minutes. Turn off the heat and stir in the spearmint. Transfer to a blender, blend until smooth, and add salt to taste. Serve warm, or pour into a shallow baking dish and refrigerate for 2 hours, until thoroughly chilled. Season with lemon juice and pepper, and serve.

saffron corn soup

Corn didn't reach Iran until the century following Columbus's first voyage, and with the exception of delicious char-grilled balal *on the cob (page 30) dipped in saltwater—a beloved street food—this newcomer is still rarely seen in Iranian cooking. But creamy, mellow corn kernels provide a perfect backdrop for hard-edged Persian ingredients, like bittersweet dried limes and earthy turmeric, and they're a heavenly combination in this bright yellow soup. Squeeze the excess cooking liquid out of the limes when you remove them from the pot, so that all of their flavor goes back into the soup. Serve warm, or chill in the refrigerator for a few hours and stir in a dollop of yogurt before serving.*

serves 4 to 6

---

3 tablespoons grapeseed oil
2 yellow onions, finely diced
1 teaspoon ground turmeric
6 large ears corn, shucked
3 dried limes, soaked in hot
    water to cover for 15 minutes

6 cups chicken stock or water
$^{1}/_{2}$ teaspoon saffron, ground and
    steeped in 1 tablespoon hot
    water (see page 15)

Sea salt and freshly ground black
    pepper
2 to 3 tablespoons freshly
    squeezed lemon juice

Heat the oil in a stockpot over medium heat and cook the onions for about 10 minutes, until they start to brown. Add the turmeric and corn. Pierce the limes with a knife or fork and add them to the pot along with their soaking water. Add the stock and bring to a boil. Cover and simmer for 15 minutes, until the corn is just tender.

Squeeze the limes against the side of the pot with a long spoon to extract their concentrated flavor before removing them from the soup. Blend half of the soup in a blender, then return it to the pot. Add the saffron and season to taste with salt and pepper. Add lemon juice to taste, and serve.

Jewish Food in Iranian Cuisine

When it comes to food, Jews and Iranians have a lot in common. In both cultures, the passing of the year is measured in sacred days, and each occasion is set apart by distinct foods, which are prepared and consumed in abundance. Perhaps because such a large percentage of Jews have roots in the former Soviet Union—Iran's once boundless neighbor to the north—both peoples famously share a love of certain foods, including raw onions, garlic, pickles, dill, beets, and anything that's crisp and brown, like *tahdig* (page 128), for example, or potato latkes.

Jews have lived in Iran for over twenty-five hundred years, making Iran's Jewish community the oldest outside of Israel. Babylon, now modern-day Iraq, was conquered by the first king of the Persian Empire, Cyrus the Great, in 539 BCE. One of Cyrus's most legendary acts was to free the enslaved Jews of Babylon and allow them to return to Israel. Cyrus even funded the rebuilding of the great temple destroyed by Nebuchadnezzar, the Babylonian king who sent the Jews into exile.

So great was Cyrus's generosity that many Jews chose to stay in Persia under this benevolent king, the now-celebrated author of the Cyrus Cylinder, what many scholars call the earliest charter of human rights. Today, some twenty thousand to twenty-five thousand Jews live in Iran. Although more Jews live in Iran than in any other Middle Eastern country outside of Israel, this is still only a fraction of the Jewish population that was there before the 1979 revolution.

Two Religions, One Cuisine

The food of Iranian Muslims and Jews is essentially the same, except that Iranian Jews don't mix butter or yogurt with meat. Conveniently, both Muslims and Jews eschew pork. On the other hand, the food of Mizrahi Jews—the Hebrew term for Jews who never left the Middle East and North Africa—has much less in common with the food of Ashkenazi Jews, those whose heritage is German and eastern European. On Passover, when most American Jews (the majority of whom are of Ashkenazi descent) make traditional favorites like gefilte fish and brisket, Iranian Jews eat *fesenjan* (page 109), and jeweled rice (page 121).

By tradition, Ashkenazi Jews will not eat rice, corn, red beans, and black-eyed peas at this holiday, but Persian Jews may eat all of these things (and are generally considered to have the better deal here!). Where Persian Jews are perhaps somewhat deprived at Passover is in the withholding of dairy products. In Iran, there are no dairy products that are certified kosher for Passover, so during that holiday, they are left out altogether. Because yogurt is such a key part of Persian cuisine, this is a significant sacrifice. At sundown on the last day of Passover, when Ashkenazi Jews indulge in leavened foods, Persian Jews celebrate by eating dairy—usually yogurt. A bowl of herbed yogurt and a platter of *sabzi khordan* (herbs) with bread and feta (page 27) would be a perfect way to conclude Passover in Mizrahi fashion. In the Menus section (page 186), you'll find menu ideas that follow the Mizrahic guidelines for Passover eating.

Celebrating Purim

Purim is one of the most meaningful holidays of the year for Persian Jews, as the story of Purim took place in Iran. The heroes of the Purim story, Queen Esther and her uncle Mordechai, are buried in the northwestern city of Hamadan, and their graves are a destination for tourists and natives alike. Just as in the United States, where Hanukkah has an outsize importance because of its proximity to Christmas, Purim in Iran gets a boost from *Norooz* (Persian New Year), the biggest Persian holiday of the year.

Purim customs mirror those of *Norooz*, so like other Iranians at this time of year, Persian Jews enjoy a feast of dishes that feature green herbs, they visit elderly relatives, and they give gifts of gold coins to the children in their families. The *mishloach manot*, or "Purim basket," is a gift of food that's sent on the day of Purim to friends, relatives, neighbors, and the needy. The tradition is based on a verse in the Book of Esther in the Old Testament stating that Purim is "an occasion for sending gifts to one another and presents to the poor." According to custom, the basket should contain at least two ready-to-eat food items. In the United States, the basket usually holds a piece of fresh fruit and a hamantasch, the iconic triangle-shaped cookie filled with jam, chocolate, nuts, prunes, or other sweet filling.

If you've ever tried baking hamantaschen yourself, you know just how difficult they are to make. A simpler stand-in for hamantaschen is the Persian *kloocheh*, a cookie stuffed with a spiced mixture of nuts and dried fruit that's made by Persian Jews at Purim. Different variations of *kloocheh* are prepared all the way from the Arabian Peninsula to eastern Europe and are linked not only to Jewish celebrations but also to the Easter holiday in Christian countries and to Ramadan in Muslim countries. The streamlined *kloocheh* recipe (page 155) that you'll find in this book is a good deal easier to make than hamantaschen, and the cookies themselves are pretty to look at, too.

Here are some recipes that would make great Purim basket "stuffers":

- Ajil-e Moshkel-gosha ("Problem Solver" Nut Mix) ~ page 36
- *Kloocheh* (Date-and-Walnut-Filled Cookies) ~ page 155
- Winter Orchard Tea ~ page 171
- Sour Cherry and Rose Preserves ~ page 185
- Nan-e Nokhodchi (Chickpea and Almond Flour Icebox Cookies) ~ page 145
- Nutty Chocolate Bark with Cardamom and Coffee ~ page 161

Although the Jewish culture that began so optimistically in ancient Persia is declining in modern Iran, the food traditions of Persian Jews continue to flourish and evolve in the expats' adopted countries like Israel and the United States. In Israel today, Iranian dishes like *baghali polo* (Rice with Fava and Dill, page 135), *ghormeh sabzi* (Green Herb and Kidney Bean Stew, page 115), and especially the Persian "matzoh ball" soup known as *gondi* (page 47) are all becoming familiar to the greater population via the many Iranian immigrants who have arrived there in the past thirty years. In the United States, a cultural barometer no less impressive than the *New York Times* has featured the Passover cooking traditions of Iranian Jews.

persian "matzoh balls" with chickpeas and chicken

gondi

Gondi—the word is a bawdy Persian expression for a certain part of the male anatomy—is a favorite food in many Iranian Jewish homes. These light, cardamom-scented dumplings look like matzoh balls, but instead of matzoh meal, they're made from ground chicken or turkey and chickpea flour. To get a clear, unclouded soup broth, cook the gondi in a separate pot of chicken stock, and then add them to the soup broth when serving. For a more casual presentation, cook the gondi in the same pot with the other soup ingredients. You can make the gondi dough the day before, and store it in the refrigerator.

makes 30 matzoh balls, and serves 6 to 8

MATZOH BALLS
2 yellow onions
1 egg
3 cloves garlic, minced
2 teaspoons ground cardamom
1 teaspoon ground turmeric
2 tablespoons grapeseed oil
Sea salt and freshly ground black
    pepper
2 cups chickpea flour

1 pound ground chicken or
    turkey
12 cups chicken or vegetable
    stock

SOUP BROTH
8 cups chicken or vegetable stock
1 large carrot, thinly sliced
2 cups cooked chickpeas
    (one 15-ounce can, drained
    and rinsed)

4 dried limes, soaked in hot
    water to cover for 15 minutes
2 cups loosely packed coarsely
    chopped fresh dill, flat-leaf
    parsley, or cilantro
Sea salt and freshly ground black
    pepper
1/4 cup freshly squeezed lemon
    juice

To make the matzoh balls, puree the onions in a food processor. Transfer to a large bowl, and whisk in the egg, garlic, cardamom, turmeric, oil, 2 teaspoons salt, and several grinds of pepper. Mix in the chickpea flour and chicken to form a thick paste. Cover and store the dough in the refrigerator for at least 4 hours, or up to 24 hours, to firm up.

Wet your hands with cold water and break off walnut-size pieces of the dough. Roll them into smooth balls, to make a total of 30 balls.

continued

In a large stockpot, bring the 12 cups stock and 2 teaspoons sea salt to a rapid boil. Carefully drop the dumplings into the stock. Turn down the heat to low, cover, and simmer for 50 minutes without opening the pot. When ready, the gondi will be firm in the center. Remove them with a slotted spoon. The cooking stock can be strained and used for the soup broth, or reserved for another use.

In a second stockpot, combine the 8 cups stock, carrot, and chickpeas and bring to a boil. Pierce the limes several times with a fork and add them to the stock along with their soaking water. Lower the heat and simmer, covered, for 15 minutes. Add the herbs and season to taste with salt and pepper. Stir in the lemon juice just before serving. Divide the *gondi* among soup bowls, ladle the broth over the top, and serve.

Vegetarian Option

Use 1 (14-ounce) package firm tofu in place of the chicken. Drain and press the tofu well, then pulse in a food processor until coarsely ground to the consistency of ground meat.

pomegranate soup

ash-e anar

Shot through with the tart ruby acid of pomegranate, this savory soup shows how the fruits and vegetables of the Iranian garden are threaded into every colorful panel of its culinary tapestry. Both the meat and vegetarian versions of this soup are fragrant and satisfying, and the flavors get better with time. When fresh herbs aren't available for the meatballs, replace them with half the amount of dried herbs.

serves 6 to 8

SOUP
3 tablespoons grapeseed oil
$^1/_2$ yellow onion, minced
2 cloves garlic, minced
$^3/_4$ cup split peas

1 teaspoon ground turmeric
2 teaspoons ground cumin
8 cups vegetable stock or water
$^1/_2$ cup pomegranate molasses

Sea salt and freshly ground black
   pepper
Seeds of 1 pomegranate
1 cup thick Greek-style yogurt

MEATBALLS
1/2 yellow onion, minced
2 cloves garlic, minced
1 pound lean ground lamb

2 heaping tablespoons minced
  flat-leaf parsley
2 heaping tablespoons minced
  cilantro

2 heaping tablespoons minced
  spearmint
2 teaspoons sea salt

To make the soup, heat the oil in a large stockpot over medium heat and cook the onion for about 10 minutes, until it starts to brown. Add the garlic, split peas, turmeric, cumin, and stock and bring to a boil. Lower the heat and simmer, partially covered, for about about 1 1/2 hours, until the peas are tender and the soup is slightly thickened.

To make the meatballs, in a large bowl, combine the lamb with the onion, garlic, and herbs. Add the salt and mix. Wet your hands and form the lamb into walnut-size balls.

When the split peas are tender, add the pomegranate molasses to the soup. Drop in the meatballs and simmer, covered, for about 20 minutes, until they're cooked through.

Season with salt and pepper. Ladle into bowls and garnish with the pomegranate seeds. Top with yogurt and serve.

Vegetarian Option

Follow the recipe as directed, omitting the meatballs. Along with the split peas, add 1/2 cup lentils, 1/2 cup dried mung beans, 1/2 cup pearled barley, and 1 large beet, peeled and diced small. Use 12 cups stock or water. When the beans and barley are tender, add the pomegranate molasses and 1 bunch chopped cilantro.

oat and mushroom soup

soup-e jo

This warming, tomato-infused soup was first prepared for me by my friend Somayeh on a frosty February day. Its bilingual name, soup-e jo, *and the heavy cream that usually enhances it suggest that it's a European import to Iran, but a shot of turmeric and a healthy dose of lime juice make it unmistakably Persian. Although typically made with barley (jo), this recipe calls for oats. Toasting the oats in the oven cuts their cooking time in half and gives them a nutty flavor.*

serves 4 to 6

1 cup steel-cut oats
3 tablespoons grapeseed oil
1 yellow onion, diced
2 cups cremini mushrooms, thinly sliced
2 cups grated carrots

1 teaspoon ground turmeric
1/2 cup tomato paste
Sea salt
5 cups vegetable stock or water, Minced fresh flat-leaf parsley, for garnish

1 cup milk, any kind
1/4 cup freshly squeezed lime juice
Freshly ground black pepper
Minced fresh flat-leaf parsley, for garnish

Preheat the oven to 350°F. Pulse the oats in a food processor for 30 seconds to break them down, then toast them on a dry baking sheet for 20 minutes, stirring occasionally. Let cool to room temperature and set aside.

Heat the oil in a medium saucepan over medium heat. Add the onion and cook for about 15 minutes, until translucent. Add the mushrooms and cook over low heat for about 10 minutes, until they've released all of their water.

Add the oats to the saucepan along with the carrots, turmeric, tomato paste, and 1 teaspoon salt. Pour in the stock and bring to a boil, then lower the heat and simmer, covered, for about 30 minutes, until the oats are very tender.

Turn off the heat and stir in the milk. The soup should be thick and creamy. Add the lime juice, season with salt and pepper, and serve garnished with parsley.

savory amaranth and turkey porridge

halim-e shir

This hearty winter breakfast soup is the Persian equivalent of congee, the comforting Asian rice porridge that features toppings as varied as peanuts, chiles, and crisp fried garlic. In this recipe, the traditional cracked wheat is replaced by the nutty New World grain amaranth, which blends naturally with the turkey and cinnamon that lends the porridge its festive flavor. This savory dish is a tasty and unexpected way to use leftover Thanksgiving turkey, too. Soak the amaranth overnight for quicker cooking, and stir often to prevent this delicate grain from sticking.

serves 4 to 6

1 1/2 cups amaranth
2 cups shredded cooked turkey
4 cups water
1 cup milk, any kind

3 tablespoons butter or unrefined coconut oil
2 teaspoons sea salt

3 tablespoons toasted sesame seeds
Ground cinnamon, for garnish
Maple or date sugar, for garnish

Combine the amaranth, turkey, and water in a medium saucepan. Bring to a boil, then lower the heat and simmer, covered, for about 30 minutes, until the amaranth is very soft.

Turn off the heat and stir in the milk, butter, and salt. Ladle the porridge into bowls for serving. Top each bowl with a sprinkling of sesame seeds, cinnamon, and maple sugar.

Vegetarian Option

Omit the turkey or replace it with an equivalent amount of cooked aduki beans or pinto beans.

cleansing spring nettle soup

In the lush northern province of Mazandaran between the Caspian Sea and the snowy Alborz Mountains, nettles are so profuse that there is even a town, Gazaneh, named for the prickly plant. Nettles, widely considered a blood tonic and a cure for hay fever, make for a nourishing and cleansing spring soup with a rich herbal flavor that's especially popular during Norooz (Persian New Year). My very light and brothy take on nettle soup calls for boiling the nettles in 10 cups of water, but I'd suggest adding a bit more, because the cooking water—also called nettle tea—makes a tasty, healthful tonic on its own. Remember that raw nettles sting, so protect your hands with sturdy rubber gloves until after they've been boiled, when the stingers have melted away. If you can't find nettles, spinach makes an excellent stand-in.

serves 6

10 cups vegetable stock or water
1 pound stinging nettles or
    spinach
2 yellow onions, finely diced
3 tablespoons grapeseed oil
4 cloves garlic, minced

1 teaspoon ground turmeric
$^1/_2$ teaspoon cayenne pepper
1 pound fresh peas or thawed
    frozen peas
1 cup loosely packed fresh
    spearmint, coarsely chopped

Sea salt and freshly ground black
    pepper
$^1/_4$ cup freshly squeezed lemon
    juice

Bring the stock to a boil in a large pot. While the stock heats, don sturdy rubber gloves and tear the nettle leaves from the stems. Wash the leaves in cold water, then add to the stock and boil for 1 minute. Drain into a colander placed over a large container to reserve the stock, and finely chop the nettles.

Rinse the pot and put it back on the stove over medium heat. Add the oil, followed by the onions, and cook for about 5 minutes, until soft. Add the garlic, turmeric, cayenne, and reserved cooking stock and bring to a boil. Lower the heat, add the nettles, and simmer for 20 minutes. Add the peas and cook for about 5 minutes, until just tender. Stir in the spearmint and season with salt and pepper. Add the lemon juice just before serving.

bean, herb, and noodle soup

ash-e reshteh

This classic Persian country-style soup can be served as a hearty starter or a full-fledged meal in itself. Feel free to substitute fava beans, navy beans, mung beans, or black-eyed peas for the beans used here. This soup gets better with time, so I recommend making it several hours or even a day ahead.

serves 6 to 8

3 yellow onions
1/2 cup grapeseed oil
2 cups cooked chickpeas
    (one 15-ounce can, drained
    and rinsed)
2 cups cooked kidney beans
    (one 15-ounce can, drained
    and rinsed)
4 cups frozen lima beans (one
    16-ounce bag)

1/2 cup lentils
4 cloves garlic, minced
1 teaspoon ground turmeric
3 heaping tablespoons dried dill
    weed
3 heaping tablespoons dried
    mint
12 cups vegetable or chicken
    stock
Sea salt

6 ounces linguine noodles,
    broken into thirds
3 cups coarsely chopped kale,
    collards, or spinach (stems
    discarded)
1/3 cup freshly squeezed lemon
    juice
1 1/2 cups thick Greek-style yogurt,
    for garnish

Dice 1 of the onions. Heat a large stockpot over medium heat and add 3 tablespoons of the oil. Add the onion and cook for 10 minutes, until it starts to brown. Add the chickpeas, kidney beans, lima beans, lentils, garlic, turmeric, dill, and 1 tablespoon of the mint. Add the stock and bring to a boil. Decrease the heat and simmer gently, covered, for 1 hour to blend the flavors.

Slice the remaining 2 onions into thin half-moons. Heat a medium skillet over high heat and add the remaining 5 tablespoons oil. Add the onions and panfry, stirring frequently, for about 10 minutes, until golden. Add the remaining 2 tablespoons mint and sauté about 2 minutes, until soft and fragrant.

In the last 30 minutes of cooking, add the noodles and leafy greens to the soup, and stir well so that the noodles don't clump. Stir in 2 teaspoons sea salt. When the noodles are tender, add the lemon juice and season to taste. Serve garnished with a large dollop of yogurt and a spoonful of the fried onions.

salads

According to Persian tradition, foods can either heat your body up or cool it down, and it's typically advised that you keep these energies carefully balanced. It's a mindset not unlike traditional Chinese medicine, but whereas the Chinese system cautions against eating raw foods because of their cooling, "aqueous" nature, Persian food philosophy makes plenty of room for good old-fashioned roughage.

Some good examples of the Persian passion for raw vegetables are the Fresh Herb Platter (page 27) in the Starters chapter, a wonderfully simple salad in the form of whole, unseasoned herbs, and the warm-weather Persian custom of dipping romaine leaves into seasoned vinegar, or *sekanjabin* (page 173). Even a snack as simple as raw pomegranates dusted with angelica seeds and a pinch of salt can be seen as a kind of salad, according to our usual understanding of a salad as something cool and crisp.

Nevertheless, the tradition of a true salad course never took hold in Iran, probably because fresh produce permeates every aspect of the daily diet, and there's arguably no need to designate a separate vegetable course. Perhaps that's why the term "salad" in Iran generally refers to things like thick Persian yogurt mixed with vegetables, such as Yogurt with Beets (page 35) and Yogurt with Shallots (page 36) in the Starters chapter. One clear exception is *Salad Shirazi* (page 59) in this chapter, which, though it doesn't contain lettuce, is absolutely a salad, even in the Western sense of the word. A medley of tomatoes and cucumbers dressed simply with lime juice and dried mint, it's a familiar dish throughout the Middle East, here interpreted in an unmistakably Persian manner.

Because salads are uncharted territory in Iranian cuisine, I've taken the opportunity to let my imagination run wild, and you'll find traditional Persian ingredients paired in surprising ways here. A few foreign interlopers also make an appearance, including celery root, corn, and strawberries. Vinegar Carrots with Toasted Sesame Seeds (page 65) takes its inspiration from China, Iran's Silk Road neighbor to the East, and the Roasted Peach and Corn Salad in Tamarind Vinaigrette (page 61) weaves in good ol' American corn. The Cucumber and Watermelon Salad (page 66), on the other hand, contains strictly traditional Persian ingredients, such as walnuts and mint. These salad recipes share a focus on seasonal produce, and they all revel in the simple truth that flavorful, fresh ingredients like pomegranates, peaches, watermelon, and rhubarb don't require a lot of fuss to taste spectacular.

chicken with potatoes and olives

Persians love French culture, and that's reflected in their favorite chicken salad known as salad olivieh, typically made with potatoes, eggs, and lots of mayonnaise. Created by a French chef in Moscow, the recipe traveled to Iran with the many immigrants who found safe haven there after the Russian Revolution. These days you'll find it on the menu of most Persian restaurants in the United States. This version, made with yogurt, green olives, and lemon juice, is less of a Franco-Russian approach and more of a Mediterranean one. Serve it plain, over salad greens, or in a sandwich stuffed with crisp lettuce leaves.

serves 6

1¹/₂ pounds fingerling potatoes or other waxy potatoes, scrubbed
Sea salt
1 tablespoon mustard seeds
1 tablespoon coriander seeds
2 teaspoons fennel seeds

3 tablespoons extra-virgin olive oil
6 tablespoons freshly squeezed lemon juice
6 scallions, green and white parts, thinly sliced
1 cup thick Greek-style yogurt

3 cups (1 pound) coarsely chopped skinless cooked chicken
1 cup pitted green olives, halved
1 cup tightly packed chopped fresh flat-leaf parsley
Freshly ground black pepper

Place the potatoes in a medium saucepan and cover with cold water. Add 2 teaspoons salt and bring to a boil, then simmer, covered, for about 25 minutes, until the potatoes are fork-tender. Drain, cool, and cut into halves or quarters, depending on their size.

Toast the mustard, coriander, and fennel seeds in a skillet over high heat for 1 minute. Let cool and grind in a spice grinder.

In a large bowl, whisk the spices with the oil, lemon juice, scallions, yogurt, and 2 teaspoons sea salt. Add the chicken and stir to coat. Fold in the potatoes, olives, and parsley. Season with salt and pepper, and serve.

Vegetarian Option

Replace the chicken with cooked chickpeas.

tomato and cucumber salad

salad shirazi

This crisp salad makes a refreshing accompaniment to heavier foods because it's dressed very simply with fresh lime juice. Use heirloom tomatoes and cucumbers in different hues when they're in season. My friend Somayeh, a graduate student in Philadelphia, taught me how to make this salad, and when I prepare it, I picture her rubbing the mint between her palms and letting it fall in a flurry of green over the vegetables.

serves 4 to 6

3 or 4 medium unwaxed cucumbers (1 pound), sliced in half lengthwise

2 medium to large tomatoes (1 pound), diced
$^1/_2$ white or yellow onion, diced
2 tablespoons dried mint

$^1/_2$ cup freshly squeezed lime juice
Sea salt and freshly ground black pepper

Seed and dice the cucumbers, and combine them with the tomatoes and onion. Hold your hands over the salad and rub the mint between your palms so that the oils in your skin activate the flavor.

Add the lime juice, season with salt and pepper, and stir gently to mix. Serve immediately.

shaved celery root and pomegranate salad

During Hannukah, it's customary to eat fried foods to commemorate the miracle of the oil that lasted for eight days and nights. According to historians, that precious substance was olive oil, which has been produced in Israel for thousands of years. In addition to fried latkes—the traditional holiday favorite—try this crisp, palate-cleansing salad that's dressed with olive oil and features Iran's most storied fruit. It's so tangy and fruity, you may even want to put it right on your latkes.

serves 6

3 tablespoons freshly squeezed lime juice

3 tablespoons extra-virgin olive oil

1 tablespoon honey

Sea salt

1 large celery root

Seeds of 2 pomegranates (see page 62)

Freshly ground black pepper

In a large salad bowl, whisk together the lime juice, olive oil, honey, and 1 teaspoon of salt.

Rinse the celery root and slice off the rough outside layer. Using the large holes on a box grater, or the grater attachment of a food processor, grate the celery root and add it to the dressing. Add the pomegranate seeds and toss until they're well coated with the dressing. Season to taste with salt and pepper, and serve.

roasted peach and corn salad in tamarind vinaigrette

Corn and peaches are among my favorite summer flavors, and I like combining them in both desserts and savory dishes, like this one. Roasting fruits and vegetables brings out their natural sugars, and that sweetness is perfectly complemented by the tart taste of tamarind. For a deliciously smoky taste, grill the corn and peaches instead of roasting them. Nectarines, apricots, and plums are all good stand-ins for the peaches.

serves 4 to 6

3 sweet, ripe peaches
3 large ears corn (2 to 3 cups kernels)
3 tablespoons grapeseed oil
Sea salt and freshly ground black pepper

1 shallot, minced
3 tablespoons Thai tamarind concentrate (see page 16), strained to remove grit

1 tablespoon white wine vinegar
2 small heads of butter lettuce, torn

Preheat the oven to 425°F.

Peel the peaches and cut the flesh into coarse chunks. Slice the kernels from the corncobs, and combine them with the peaches in a large bowl. Add 2 tablespoons of the oil, $1/2$ teaspoon salt, and a pinch of pepper, and toss well. Spread the peaches and corn on a baking sheet, and bake, stirring every 10 minutes, for 20 to 30 minutes, until the corn begins to brown and the peaches are very soft. Cool slightly.

While the peaches and corn roast, make the dressing. In a serving bowl, combine the shallot, tamarind, vinegar, and the remaining 1 tablespoon oil. Season with 1 teaspoon salt, and marinate until the corn and peaches are done.

Add the lettuce to the dressing, followed by the warm peaches and corn, and toss to coat. Season to taste with salt and pepper, then serve.

How to Open a Pomegranate

If you buy a pomegranate,
buy one whose ripeness
has caused it to be cleft open
with a seed-revealing smile.
Its laughter is a blessing,
for through its wide-open mouth
it shows its heart . . .

—Rumi, *Mathnawi 1*, translated by
Kabir Helminski and Ahmad Rezwani

The sensuous pomegranate is an ancient Persian ingredient and an iconic part of its cuisine. One of my favorite things about teaching Persian cooking classes is giving people their first taste of a pomegranate. There's a look of puzzled delight when they bite down on the tart, juicy arils (seeds) and hit the pith at the center. I'm frequently asked, "Do I eat the whole thing or spit it out?" My answer is always, "Eat the whole thing!"

Before eating the pomegranate, though, you have to get it open and extract the seeds from the lacy white pith in which they're embedded. Ideally, you'd like to do this without spraying yourself and your entire kitchen with the pomegranate's sticky red juice, which is known to stain clothes. The successful accomplishment of this operation is a topic shrouded in mystery and confusion, but here are a few tried-and-true methods.

Fruit Platter Method

My cousin Ali, who is an excellent—and very technical—cook, showed me this method of preparing pomegranate sections for a fruit platter. Using a very sharp or a serrated knife, slice off both the crown and stem ends of the

pomegranate, then cut off the rind the way you would peel the skin from an apple, starting at the top and working your way around and down. Now, at the top of the pomegranate you can see six seams that separate the pomegranate into six sections. Starting at a seam, make a shallow incision with your knife and drag it all the way down

to the bottom of the pomegranate. Repeat at each seam, then gently break apart the sections. Peel off any membrane still clinging to the fruit, and break the sections in half or leave them intact. They will be roughly triangular in shape. Serve like orange sections. (See photo sequence below and at left.)

Juice Method

Firmly roll an unpeeled pomegranate around on a cutting board, feeling the seeds break inside the skin. When you've rolled the entire fruit and it feels soft all over, put it in the sink and cut a small circle out of the skin. Bring the fruit to your mouth and suck out the juice.

Spoon Method

Hold the pomegranate on its side on a cutting board, with the crown and stem ends facing north and south. Slice the pomegranate in half vertically. Turn the halves cut side up and make four or five shallow incisions, about 1 inch in length, around the cut edge of the fruit. Loosely hold a pomegranate half from the bottom, cut side down, so that your palm is touching the seeds. Over a large, deep bowl, bang the skin firmly with the back of a heavy spoon to knock out the seeds. Repeat with the remaining half.

Water Method

Fill a large bowl halfway with cold water. Slice off the crown and stem ends of the pomegranate. Stand the pomegranate on one of the flat ends, and divide the fruit into quarters by slicing four shallow incisions in the skin from the top to the bottom. Break the fruit into quarters. Submerge the fruit in the water and pull out the seeds. The seeds will sink, while the pith and skin float to the top. As soon as you've seeded all four quarters, skim the waste off the top, and pour the seeds into a sieve.

vinegar carrots with toasted sesame seeds

This pungent salad is great as a sandwich fixing on the Sweet and Smoky Beet Burgers (page 79), or tucked into flatbread with the Potato Cakes with Tamarind Sauce (page 81). Use a carrot peeler to peel the carrots into long, graceful ribbons or a mandoline slicer to cut them into matchsticks. To peel the carrots easily, lay them on a cutting board, hold onto the stem end, and rotate as you peel away each section. Marinate the salad for a few hours before serving to let the nutty toasted sesame oil infuse the carrots.

serves 4

1/2 cup sesame seeds (white or black)
1 clove garlic, minced
2 tablespoons white vinegar
2 tablespoons rice vinegar

1 tablespoon honey
1 tablespoon toasted sesame oil
1 teaspoon red pepper flakes
Sea salt

1 1/2 pounds carrots, cut lenthwise into thin ribbons
1 cup tightly packed fresh cilantro

Heat a small skillet over medium-high heat. When hot, add the sesame seeds and alternate between shaking the pan and stirring the seeds. When the seeds start to pop, after a couple of minutes, transfer them to a plate and let cool to room temperature.

In a small bowl, whisk together the garlic, vinegars, honey, sesame oil, red pepper flakes, sesame seeds, and 1 teaspoon salt. Pour the dressing over the carrots, add the cilantro, and toss well. Season to taste with salt and serve.

cucumber and watermelon salad

Sweet, thirst-quenching watermelon is one of Iran's most bountiful and well-loved fruits. On scalding summer days, its juice is a refreshing balm in both the dusty desert and in Tehran's smoggy city streets, where watermelons are sold whole or by the slice. Even the seeds are roasted and eaten as a snack. At the observance of Shab-e Yalda *on December 21, the longest night of the year, it's customary to share a watermelon with friends and family, in the anticipation of an auspicious new year. You can assemble this crisp, juicy salad ahead of time, and add the salt and vinegar just before serving.*

serves 4

1 pound unwaxed cucumbers,
 sliced in half lengthwise
3 cups diced seedless
 watermelon

1 scallion, green part only, thinly
 sliced
3/4 teaspoon sea salt
1 tablespoon white wine vinegar

Seed the cucumbers and cut them into half-moons 1/2 inch thick. In a bowl, combine the cucumbers with the watermelon and scallion. Add the salt and vinegar, mix well, and serve immediately.

radish, rhubarb, and strawberry salad

According to Persian folklore, the first man and woman sprang forth from the rosy red stalks of the rhubarb plant. Although Americans tend to think of it as a fruit, rhubarb is a vegetable, mainly used in Iranian cooking to add sourness to savory dishes. Strawberries, which came to Persia from the West, are known as toot farangi, *or "foreign berry," and in this lively salad they temper the rhubarb's acidic edge. Spicy radishes complete this scarlet trio, while a scattering of pistachios lends it a dramatic finish. Once dressed, serve the salad immediately.*

serves 4

2 tablespoons balsamic vinegar
3 tablespoons extra-virgin
   olive oil
1 clove garlic, finely minced
4 cups loosely packed torn salad
   greens

1 large handful fresh spearmint
Sea salt and freshly ground black
   pepper
1 rhubarb stalk, thinly shaved
5 radishes, thinly shaved

1 cup strawberries, hulled and
   quartered
Toasted pistachios, for garnish

In a large bowl, whisk 1 tablespoon of the vinegar and 2 tablespoons of the oil with the garlic. Add the greens and mint and toss to coat. Season with salt and pepper, and portion onto plates.

In the same bowl, combine the rhubarb, radishes, and strawberries. Drizzle with the remaining 1 tablespoon vinegar and 1 tablespoon oil, and season with salt and pepper. Mix well and spoon over the greens. Top with the pistachios, and serve immediately.

vegetable and egg entrées

Persians have what you might call an infatuation with produce. In Iran, a food as simple as a boiled beet, a raw cucumber, or an unripe almond can inspire poetry. Aside from the ubiquitous kebab, meat generally plays a supporting role in any given dish and is a bit player compared to the grains, greens, legumes, vegetables, and fruits that dominate the cuisine. It has even been argued that ancient Iran may at one time have been a vegetarian society.

In light of the many vegetarian cultures that still exist along the Silk Road—the Hindus and Jains in India, the Buddhists in China and Tibet—the idea of a primarily plant-eating Persia is hardly out of the question. In the epic poem the *Shahnameh* (Book of Kings), the eleventh-century Persian poet Ferdowsi recounts the story of the first time the ancient Persians ate animal flesh. In the poem, the devil seduces the mighty King Zahhak by feeding him meat, precipitating his downfall.

With ingredients sourced from throughout the Persian Empire and trading partners in southern Europe, northern Africa, and the Far East, the ancient Persians would have had a colorful diet based on the sheer variety of edible plants alone, and that diversity continues to this day. Throughout this book you'll find recipes that pay homage to the vibrant Persian vegetable bazaar, and in this chapter alone you'll find green herbs, artichokes, garlic, onions, tomatoes, beets, potatoes, and more.

You'll also find vegetable dishes based on time-honored Persian cooking traditions, as well as my own newfangled creations that incorporate Persian staples. The Sweet and Smoky Beet Burger (page 79), for example, is my original take on the veggie burger, made with Persian-approved ingredients, such as walnuts, golden raisins, and kidney beans. The Herb Frittata with Walnuts and Rose Petals (page 71), on the other hand, is a popular Persian baked egg dish called a *kuku*. Like the Spanish *tortilla* or the Italian frittata, you can add just about anything to a *kuku*, but it typically features one main ingredient, such as eggplant, cauliflower, chicken, or green herbs. The Potato Cakes with Tamarind Sauce (page 81) in this chapter are what's known as a *kotlet*, a Persian favorite similar to a Russian *kotlety*, a hearty patty made with minced meat or vegetables.

You already know about kebabs, but the kebabs in this chapter are made of animal-free (but perfectly "meaty") tempeh and seasoned with a citrusy herb marinade. Stuffed vegetables, called *dolmeh*, come in all shapes and sizes in Persian cuisine and are usually filled with vegetables and meat. In these recipes, they come in the form of Roasted Stuffed Artichokes with Mint Oil (page 73) and the Stuffed Tomatoes (page 76) filled with quinoa, goat cheese, white beans, and parsley. What these varied dishes have in common is their uniquely Persian seasoning. Turmeric, cinnamon, lime, caramelized onions, and lemony sumac give these vegetarian foods a depth of flavor that is rich, exotic, and delightfully unexpected.

herb frittata with walnuts and rose petals

kuku sabzi

Slicing into this fragrant frittata reveals an emerald-green interior with a bready texture and a warm, nutty flavor. This springtime dish, full of green herbs that signify new beginnings, is part of the traditional meal at Norooz, the Persian New Year that falls on the spring equinox. Try folding slices of the frittata into flatbread with the feta, radishes, and herbs on the Fresh Herb Platter (page 27).

It's important that the herbs are thoroughly dry, as water will make the texture of the frittata spongy. It can be made the day before serving and will last for a few days.

serves 6

3 tablespoons grapeseed oil
1/2 cup finely ground walnuts
2 teaspoons crushed dried rose petals or dried whole rosebuds pulled apart and stems removed

2 cloves garlic, minced
About 2 cups loosely packed fresh flat-leaf parsley, finely chopped
About 2 cups loosely packed fresh cilantro, finely chopped

1 bunch scallions, green and white parts, finely chopped
Sea salt and freshly ground black pepper
7 eggs, whisked

Preheat the oven to 350°F.

Heat an 8- to 10-inch ovenproof skillet over medium heat. Add the oil, followed by the walnuts, rose petals, and garlic and cook for a few minutes until the ingredients start to release their fragrance. Add the herbs and scallions and cook for about 2 minutes, until wilted. Turn off the heat and season with salt and pepper. Let the pan cool for a few minutes, then gently stir in the eggs.

Transfer the skillet to the oven and bake for 15 minutes, until the center of the frittata springs back when lightly pressed. To unmold, loosen the edge with a butter knife and invert onto a serving platter. Serve hot or cold.

roasted stuffed artichokes with mint oil

Mellow, bittersweet artichokes have a wild relative in cardoons, which are similar in taste but require hours of soaking and simmering to become edible. Cardoons have been eaten in the Middle East since biblical times and are much loved in Iran. With the flavors of mint and saffron and a scoop of fluffy ricotta filling, this dish takes its inspiration both from Persian cardoon cookery and from the flavors of Italy, one of the first European countries to embrace the artichoke wholeheartedly. Serve the artichokes in shallow bowls, along with bread to sop up the pan juice.

serves 2 as a main course

1 lemon
2 globe artichokes
1/2 cup freshly squeezed lemon juice
1 tablespoon dried mint
1/4 cup grapeseed oil

1 clove garlic, finely minced
Sea salt
2 ounces ricotta cheese, drained
Pinch of saffron, ground and steeped in 1 tablespoon hot water (see page 15)

Grated zest of 1 lemon
1 egg, whisked
Freshly ground black pepper

Preheat the oven to 450°F.

Fill a medium bowl three-quarters full with cold water. Cut the lemon in half, squeeze the juice into the water, and throw in the rind.

Slice off the top third of 1 artichoke with a serrated knife, and cut off the stem to make a flat base. Pull off the small leaves around the bottom, and snip the tips of the remaining leaves with scissors. Stretch open the center of the artichoke with your thumbs, and pluck out the inner yellow leaves. Pull out the purple choke, and scrape out the fibrous hairs with a melon baller, a grapefruit spoon, or a paring knife. Place it in the lemon water to prevent browning, and repeat with the remaining artichoke.

In a medium bowl, whisk the lemon juice with the mint, oil, and garlic. Add a pinch of salt, and set aside for a few minutes to allow the mint to soften.

continued

Whisk together the ricotta, saffron, and lemon zest in a small bowl, and season to taste with salt and pepper. Mix in the egg. Spoon the ricotta into the center of the artichokes.

Place the artichokes in a rimmed baking dish. Pour the mint oil over the artichokes, drizzling it on the outer leaves as well as the filling. Add a splash of water to the baking dish, and cover tightly. Roast the artichokes for $1^1/_2$ hours, until the flesh is very tender and the ricotta is firm and doubled in size.

Serve warm, topped with the pan juice. To eat an artichoke, pull off the leaves and dip the fleshy part in the pan juice. When you reach the center, cut into the ricotta and the artichoke heart with a fork.

Islam at the Dinner Table

While Iran has been a Muslim country for more than a thousand years, it was only in the sixteenth century that Iran's ruling Safavid Dynasty officially declared its allegiance to the Shia sect of Islam. Until that time, Iran had been principally Sunni, like most of its Arab neighbors and like the majority of Muslims throughout the world.

So what sets Shia Muslims apart from Sunnis? The break between the two sects came some fourteen hundred years ago, when the Prophet Mohammed died. One group of the prophet's followers believed that leadership of the community should pass to Ali, the prophet's cousin and son-in-law, and these people became the Shiites. A larger group, who would become the Sunnis, wanted the prophet's friend Abu Bakr to lead. The Sunnis succeeded in electing Abu Bakr to the role of *caliph*, or supreme ruler of the Islamic empire, and although Ali eventually became the fourth elected caliph, he was assassinated, and the Sunnis won out once again. When Ali's son Hussein—the prophet's grandson—came of age, he tried to take back the caliphate, but he was killed in battle in Karbala, Iraq, by the Sunnis. Hussein became a martyr, and his death is commemorated yearly in Iran on the day of *Ashura*, when passion plays reenact the details of his demise, and men whip themselves in street processions in a ritual show of grief.

Still, like all Iranian holidays, Ashura is observed with celebratory eating. On the street, food is freely distributed in what resembles a giant outdoor festival stretching across neighborhoods, with candles lighting the way to huge vats of delicious Persian stew, which is spooned into hundreds of bowls for strangers and friends alike. The traditional foods served include *gheimeh* stew of lamb and split peas, rice or *adas polo* (rice with lentils), chicken, *sholeh zard* rice pudding (page 157), and tea. Known collectively as *nazri*, these foods take on a special significance on Ashura, and are thought to bring blessings and fulfill wishes for those who prepare and eat them.

Along with their Sunni neighbors, Shiites celebrate the holy month of Ramadan, the ninth month of the Islamic calendar. At Ramadan, Muslims fast throughout the daylight hours, in observance of the holy days when the words of the Koran were revealed to the prophet Muhammad. Interestingly, the date of Ramadan is not fixed, but travels the length of the calendar, moving eleven days earlier each year. According to tradition, it's permitted to eat before dawn and after sunset, but between these hours even drinking water is discouraged.

The predawn meal during Ramadan is a very early breakfast eaten in the dark, called the *sahari*. For sahari, Iranians eat cold foods prepared beforehand, like the baked egg dish *Kuku Sabzi* (page 71), *kufteh* rice meatballs (page 88), flatbread, cheese, eggs, tea, and dates. Dinner, eaten after sundown, is called *iftar*. At sunset, the fast is broken with a glass of warm water or milk accompanied by a sweet date, the food eaten by Mohammad to break his fasts in the Koran. After that, iftar dinner is often a bowl of nourishing and hearty soup like *Ash-e reshteh* (page 53) or *Halim* (page 51), while dessert is sticky-sweet *zulbia* and *bamieh*, two kinds of deep-fried pastries covered in sugar syrup.

Ramadan's festive finale, *Eid ul-Fitr*, begins with the sighting of the new moon, and marks the end of a month of fasting. Eid is a time for elaborate feasting. Because the placement of Ramadan in the calendar changes from one year to the next, the holiday has no seasonality and therefore no specific food is attached to Eid. But this is an occasion for good cooks to outdo themselves, and you can always expect that the Eid meal will be impressive and include plenty of sweet treats to make up for four weeks of self-denial.

stuffed tomatoes with pistachio pesto

In these savory stuffed tomatoes, a lemony pistachio pesto melts into quinoa, tender white beans, and goat cheese. Make these tomatoes when you have leftover quinoa on hand, and serve them with flatbread and a simple green salad.

serves 4

---

4 medium heirloom or beefsteak
   tomatoes
$^1/_3$ cup pistachios
4 scallions, green and white
   parts, coarsely chopped
1 cup tightly packed fresh flat-leaf
   parsley, plus extra for garnish

Zest of 1 lemon
3 tablespoons freshly squeezed
   lemon juice
Sea salt
3 tablespoons grapeseed oil
3 cloves garlic, minced
1 heaping cup cooked quinoa

$^1/_2$ cup cooked white beans,
   rinsed and drained
$^1/_3$ pound chèvre-style goat
   cheese, crumbled
Freshly ground black pepper
Sumac, for garnish

Preheat the oven to 425°F.

Slice off the top $^1/_2$ inch of the tomatoes, and scoop out the insides (save the tomato scraps to add to soups and stews). Place the tomatoes close together in a rimmed baking dish.

In a food processor, combine the pistachios, scallions, parsley, lemon zest and juice, and 1 teaspoon salt. Pulse several times to form a coarse pesto.

Heat 2 tablespoons of the oil in a skillet over medium heat. Add the garlic and cook until fragrant, about a minute. Add the quinoa and beans and sauté over low heat for 10 minutes, until the garlic has mellowed. Stir in the pesto, and cook for about 5 minutes, until the mixture is heated through and fairly dry. Season with salt and pepper. Turn off the heat and fold in the goat cheese.

Spoon the mixture into the tomatoes, filling them just above the rim. Drizzle with the remaining 1 tablespoon of oil, and roast for about 25 minutes, until the filling on top is golden.

Carefully transfer the tomatoes onto a plate. If they've become very tender, you may need a couple of large spoons to move them without breaking. To serve, garnish with a sprinkling of sumac and a few torn parsley leaves.

A Savory Prescription for Health

The true nature of Persian cuisine is fresh, unprocessed, and vegetable-centric, with a variety of ingredients that are carefully balanced within virtually every recipe and menu. The Persian diet leans toward the same heart-healthy, low-cholesterol guidelines that all Mediterranean diets do, but Iranians are perhaps more enthusiastic about their vegetables than other cultures—after all, this is a land where boiled beets are among the most beloved of street foods!

Vegetables, both cooked and raw, are eaten daily in Persian homes. When guests come to visit, it's typical for Iranians to put out a bowl of fresh fruit studded with small, sweet cucumbers and cherry tomatoes. Most Persian meals are accompanied by a platter of *sabzi khordan*, "herbs for eating," laid with piles of fragrant mint, chives, basil, dill, fenugreek, cilantro, tarragon, and parsley, along with feta cheese and flatbread. You might even say that Persians are infatuated with green herbs; at *Norooz* (Persian New Year), it's customary to serve an entire dinner devoted to them.

Contrary to popular belief, meat is traditionally used in modest quantities, as native philosophy stipulates that eating too much of it can throw the body off balance. In fact, kebabs are not a typical Persian meal, but are generally considered restaurant food. The reason kebabs have come to represent Persian cooking to so many people, it's argued, is because women are masters of the more complex stews and rice dishes and kebabs are easy-to-make "dude food." Since women do the cooking at home and men cook in public in restaurants, tourists who eat exclusively in restaurants don't know that there is so much more to Persian food than kebabs! In fact, most Iranians consider a home-cooked meal far superior to one that's cooked in a restaurant. Yes, there are some great Iranian restaurants out there, but what you really want is an invitation to dine in a Persian home—or to do the cooking yourself.

A protein you will see a lot of in Persian homes is the humble bean. Inexpensive and full of vitamins, beans are eaten almost daily. As in Indian cuisine, they are usually cooked with turmeric to help make them more digestible. Another source of protein is nuts, which contain unsaturated fat and are linked to the prevention of heart disease. Pistachios and walnuts are native to Iran, while almonds come from nearby in the Middle East, so Iranians have had eons to integrate them into their food. Popular Persian snacks include creamy fresh walnuts soaked in saltwater and crunchy green almonds eaten fresh from the pod.

Although Iranians love rich ingredients like nuts, Persian food is generally low in cholesterol. There are few dairy products used in Persian cooking, with the exception of *panir*, a fresh white cheese similar to feta, and yogurt, which is easy to digest and full of beneficial bacteria.

Persians rarely eat dessert. Of course, for special occasions both store-bought and homemade pastries are served, but the typical way to end a Persian meal is with nuts and fruit. Maybe it's because Iran has such a long history as an agrarian country and remains one of the world's leading producers of fruit, but Persians have a genuine sweet tooth for juicy, pungent fruits like watermelon, pomegranates, grapes, cherries, oranges, and tangerines. Stores specializing in dried fruits and nuts are as popular in Iran as pastry and candy shops are in America, but instead of doughnuts and chocolate bars, Iran's "sweet shops" feature jewel-toned dried fruits like figs, raisins, mulberries, lemons, peaches, mangoes, and, of course, dates.

sweet and smoky beet burgers

These scarlet burgers can be served on top of grains or salad, eaten like latkes or falafel, or tucked into a bun. Top them with any of the dips and spreads in the Starters and Snacks chapter, the Tamarind Date Chutney (page 183), or the Fig Mustard (page 182). My favorite way to eat them is topped with yogurt, a fragrant mound of dill, and the Tomato and Cucumber Salad (page 59). The burger mixture can be made a day ahead and stored in the refrigerator.

makes 8 burgers

1 yellow onion
3 tablespoons grapeseed oil, plus extra for searing
1 cup peeled and grated beets (approximately 1 small beet)
3 cloves garlic, crushed

1 cup walnuts
1/2 cup golden raisins
2 teaspoons sweet smoked paprika
1/2 cup cooked green lentils, rinsed and drained

Sea salt and freshly ground black pepper
2 cups cooked short-grain brown rice or white sushi rice, at room temperature
1 egg

Slice the onion to a thickness of 1/4 inch. In a medium skillet, sauté the onion in the oil over medium-high heat for 10 to 15 minutes, until it starts to darken and caramelize. Turn down the heat slightly and add the beets along with the garlic, walnuts, raisins, and paprika, and cook for 10 minutes, stirring often.

Transfer the contents of the skillet to a food processor and pulse several times until chunky. In a large bowl, combine the onion mixture with the lentils, 2 teaspoons salt, and 1 teaspoon pepper. Replace the food processor without washing and add the rice and egg, and pulse to form a coarse puree. Add the rice mixture to the onion-lentil mixture and mix well with your hands.

Lightly oil your hands and divide the dough into 8 portions. Shape each portion into a patty just under 1 inch thick.

Heat a heavy-bottomed skillet over medium-high heat and add oil to coat the bottom. Place the burgers in the skillet and cook undisturbed for 5 minutes. Gently flip the burgers and turn down the heat to low. Cover and cook for 10 minutes, until the burgers have a firm, brown crust. Serve hot with your favorite condiments.

tempeh kebabs with minty cilantro-lime sauce

Smoke-kissed kebabs are Iran's beloved contribution to street food the world over. From the African suya kebab *seasoned with ground peanuts to the Chinese* chuanr *made with anything from grasshoppers to starfish, everyone has taken to "the stick." These tempeh kebabs gush with the char-grilled tastes of lime, sumac, garlic, and mint. Tempeh has a great texture for grilling, but its base flavor is bland, so marinating the kebabs overnight, or even for a couple of days, makes all the difference in putting the flavor of this vegetarian kebab over the top.*

makes about 10 (8-inch) skewers

5 scallions, green and white parts, minced
1/2 cup grapeseed oil
1/2 cup freshly squeezed lime juice
1/2 teaspoon ground turmeric

3 cloves garlic, minced
Sea salt and freshly ground black pepper
2 (8-ounce) packages tempeh, cut into 1 1/2-inch cubes
1 pint cherry tomatoes

1 cup loosely packed fresh spearmint
1 cup loosely packed fresh cilantro
1/3 cup plain yogurt (not thick)
2 tablespoons sumac, for garnish

Whisk together the scallions, oil, lime juice, turmeric, and garlic with 1 tablespoon salt and 2 teaspoons pepper. Add the tempeh and toss to coat. Transfer to a rimmed baking dish and marinate in the refrigerator, covered, for at least 1 hour or up to 2 days.

If using wooden or bamboo skewers, soak them in salty water for a couple of hours before grilling. Thread the tempeh onto the skewers about 1/4 inch apart, along with a few tomatoes on each skewer, leaving 2 inches of space at one end. Reserve 1/4 cup of the remaining marinade for basting, and pour the rest into a blender. Add the mint, cilantro, and yogurt. Blend until smooth to make a sauce, then season with salt.

Prepare a hot grill.

Grill the skewers, basting a few times with the reserved marinade, for 4 to 5 minutes per side, until the tempeh begins to char. Transfer the skewers to a serving platter and spoon a generous amount of the sauce over the tempeh. Put the rest in a bowl for dipping. Serve hot, garnished with the sumac.

potato cakes with tamarind sauce

kotlet

Derived from the Russian dish kotlety, a pan-fried ground meat patty, this comforting snack food will fill your kitchen with the fragrant aroma of garlic, onions, and coriander. The simple tamarind sauce gives the cakes a tangy finish. The kotlet can be eaten with a knife and fork, or stuffed into a sandwich like a veggie burger.

makes 15 cakes

1 (8-ounce) package tempeh
3 cloves garlic, minced
1 yellow onion, finely diced
1 teaspoon ground turmeric
2 tablespoons ground coriander
2 cups coarsely mashed potatoes, at room temperature

1 cup tightly packed fresh cilantro, minced
Sea salt
1 teaspoon freshly ground black pepper
2 eggs, whisked

Refined coconut oil or other high-heat oil (see page 18), for frying
$^1/_4$ cup Thai tamarind concentrate (see page 16), strained to remove grit
3 tablespoons organic cane sugar
$^1/_4$ teaspoon ground ginger

Preheat the oven to 350°F. Line a baking sheet with parchment paper.

Cut the tempeh into quarters, and pulse it a few times in a food processor until it has the texture of ground meat. In a large bowl, combine the tempeh, garlic, onion, turmeric, and coriander. Add the mashed potatoes, cilantro, 2 teaspoons salt, the pepper, and eggs, and mix to form the dough. Form into 15 patties $^3/_4$ inch thick, using $^1/_3$ cup of dough for each patty.

Heat a large skillet over medium-high heat and add oil to a depth of $^1/_4$ inch. When the oil is hot, place several cakes in the skillet, without crowding. Fry for 4 minutes per side, until golden, and drain on paper towels. Repeat with the remaining patties. Transfer the patties to the prepared baking sheet and bake for 25 minutes, in order to cook the inside.

Whisk the tamarind with the sugar, ginger, and $^1/_4$ teaspoon salt. Serve the cakes hot or at room temperature, and drizzle with the tamarind sauce. Leftover cakes will keep for up to 3 days in the refrigerator.

meat and fish entrées

Today, when people think of Persian food, kebabs are the first image that comes to mind, and with good reason. By most accounts, kebabs originated in Iran. According to legend, Persian soldiers and nomads discovered that cooking small chunks of meat over a fire was fast and fuel-efficient. Their popularity has since spread to nearly every corner of the world, including the United States, where they're a barbecue mainstay. Still, when it comes to the subject of meat in Persian cooking, kebabs are only a small part of the picture.

Historical records indicate that the ancient Persians consumed many different kinds of meat, including ox, goat, gazelle, duck, goose, pigeon, and ostrich. These animals were traditionally roasted whole, often stuffed with nuts, fruit, and herbs. In modern times, turkey, duck, chicken, and red meat all find their way into stews, rice, and the elaborately seasoned meatballs known as *kofteh*. Fish and shrimp from the Persian Gulf have always been a high point of the cuisine as well, and up until recently, the Caspian Sea was known the world over both for fresh fish and, most famously, glossy black sturgeon caviar, now sadly depleted. At *Norooz*, in fact, it's fish—not red meat—that's featured on the menu.

In this chapter, I'll walk you through a sampling of meat and fish dishes inspired by different regions of Iran. You'll find a variety of options here, including two elegant renditions of whole roasted fish: one topped with brilliant slices of caramelized oranges (page 99), the other stuffed with nuts and herbs (page 90). For the adventurous eater who is ready for full cultural immersion, there is a recipe for Grilled Liver with Cumin, Garlic, and Fresh Basil (page 96), a popular Iranian street food. Even if you *think* you don't like liver, buy some fresh, organic chicken or even lamb liver and try making this just once!

The two dishes inspired by Iran's western neighbor Turkey are the herbaceous Olive Oil–Poached Fish (page 93) and the grilled shrimp seasoned with dried lime powder and served with a garlicky parsley sauce (page 87). The Turmeric Chicken with Sumac and Lime (page 103) is an easy weeknight recipe for succulent, full-flavored chicken, and the Lamb Meatballs (page 88) are straight-up Silk Road comfort food.

And of course, there are kebab recipes for lamb, chicken, and fish, all of which have delicate marinades made from aromatic ingredients like pomegranate syrup, sumac, and turmeric. When preparing kebabs, keep in mind the Persian tradition of serving them with flatbread, because it comes in handy for pulling the grilled meat from the skewer without getting your hands messy. If you're using wooden or bamboo skewers, as opposed to metal, soak them in salty water for a couple of hours before grilling to prevent them from burning. Add enough salt so that the soaking water tastes like briny seawater— this will help to flavor the kebabs from the inside. Fire up your grill, stove, or oven, and let's get cooking!

chile-saffron fish kebabs

kebab-e mahi

In Iran, fish dishes are plentiful in the north near the Caspian Sea. But they take on a different character entirely in the south of the country near the Persian Gulf, where the cuisine is influenced by the flavors of nearby Africa, where tamarind originates, and India, Iran's hot chile–loving neighbor to the east. This recipe calls for relatively mild jalapeño chiles, but you can use any hot chile that you prefer—try habaneros or sweet red Anaheims. The natural oils in chiles can cling to your hands and burn if you rub your eyes, so wash your hands well after cutting them (you may even want to wear gloves when working with very hot varieties).

serves 4

1 1/2 pounds skinless, firm-fleshed fish, such as Pacific halibut, striped bass, or albacore tuna, cut into 1-inch pieces
Sea salt and freshly ground black pepper

1/2 yellow onion, minced
2 cloves garlic, minced
2 jalapeño chiles, seeded and minced
1/4 cup freshly squeezed lime juice

1/2 teaspoon saffron, ground and steeped in 2 teaspoons hot water (see page 15)
1/4 cup plain yogurt (not thick)
Cilantro, for garnish
Sumac, for garnish

If using wooden or bamboo skewers, soak them in salty water for a couple of hours before grilling. Thread the fish onto skewers 1/4 inch apart, leaving 2 inches of space at the end. Season the kebabs with salt and pepper, and place them on a rimmed baking sheet.

Whisk together the onion, garlic, chiles, lime juice, saffron, and yogurt, and season to taste with salt and pepper. Pour the sauce over the kebabs, and toss gently.

Prepare a hot grill.

Oil the grill, lay the skewers on the grill, and cook for 3 minutes per side, until the fish is just cooked through in the center. Serve, garnished with cilantro and sumac.

Vegetarian Option

Use extra-firm tofu in place of the fish. Before cooking, drain the tofu and press it under a heavy weight for 1 hour, to press out as much water as possible. Let the kebabs marinate in the sauce for 1 hour before grilling.

grilled shrimp with lime powder and parsley–olive oil sauce

This rustic Turkish-style parsley sauce unlocks not only the flavor of seafood but of grains, vegetables, and chicken, too. The shrimp get a dose of intense citrus flavor from bittersweet dried lime powder. If you have dried limes, you can grind them in an electric spice grinder to make your own lime powder. You can also substitute the zest and juice of 2 to 3 fresh limes, if necessary. Use a good-quality extra-virgin olive oil in the sauce, and serve with rice or another grain.

serves 4

2 cups tightly packed fresh flat-leaf parsley
6 cloves garlic, minced
3 tablespoons freshly squeezed lemon juice

³/₄ cup good-quality extra-virgin olive oil
Sea salt
2 teaspoons dried lime powder
2 tablespoons grapeseed oil
Freshly ground black pepper

2 pounds jumbo shrimp, peeled and deveined
2 cups warm freshly cooked rice or whole grain, such as millet, quinoa, or freekeh

Coarsely chop the parsley and place it in a large bowl with the garlic, lemon juice, and extra-virgin olive oil, and stir to combine. Season to taste by adding ¹/₂ teaspoon salt at a time, until the flavors pop. Add pepper to taste.

Prepare a hot grill.

In a large bowl, whisk together the lime powder, grapeseed oil, 1 teaspoon salt, and a few grinds of pepper. Add the shrimp and toss to coat evenly. Grill the shrimp for 5 to 6 minutes on each side, until they're opaque in the middle.

Spoon the shrimp over the rice and season to taste with salt and pepper. Top with the parsley sauce and serve immediately.

Vegetarian Option

In place of the shrimp, use tempeh cut crosswise into bars ³/₄ inch wide. Increase the amount of grapeseed oil to 3 tablespoons, and season the tempeh to taste with salt and pepper before grilling.

lamb meatballs with mint and garlic

kufteh

Persians make all kinds of kufteh, or "pounded meat" delicacies, from plate-size, cinnamon-scented Tabrizi meatballs to small curried meatballs made with chickpea flour and dill. Kufteh are made with rice, which gives them a tender, fluffy texture. Before making the meatballs, it's important to soak the rice for 1 hour; otherwise, the grains won't cook through. You can combine the meat and seasonings a day before cooking, or you can cook the meatballs completely the day before and warm them in the oven the next day. Serve with Torshi (Mixed Vegetable Pickle, page 178), flatbread, yogurt, and a light salad, such as the Shaved Celery Root and Pomegranate Salad (page 60).

makes about 30 meatballs

MEATBALLS
$^1/_2$ cup basmati rice, soaked in
    cold water for 1 hour
4 cloves garlic, crushed
3 tablespoons dried mint, or
    1 cup loosely packed fresh
    spearmint
$^1/_2$ large yellow onion
1 pound ground turkey, lamb,
    or beef

1 egg, whisked
2 teaspoons sea salt
1 teaspoon freshly ground black
    pepper
Grapeseed oil, for browning the
    meatballs

SAUCE
Grapeseed oil, for frying,
    if needed
$^1/_2$ large yellow onion, diced
$^1/_2$ cup tomato paste
1 teaspoon dried dill weed
$^1/_2$ teaspoon ground cinnamon
$^1/_2$ teaspoon ground turmeric
3 cups water, boiling
Sea salt and freshly ground
    black pepper
$^1/_4$ cup freshly squeezed
    lemon juice

To make the meatballs, rinse the rice under cold water until the water runs clear, then shake off as much excess water as possible. In a food processor, combine the rice with the garlic, mint, and onion, and pulse until coarsely ground. Transfer to a large bowl and add the meat, egg, salt, and pepper. Mix well. The mixture should be pliable and easy to shape. You can cover the mixture and refrigerate for 24 hours, if desired.

Form the meat into balls the size of a heaping tablespoon. Heat a large skillet over medium heat and add enough oil to coat the bottom. Working in batches, cook the meatballs for 6 to 8 minutes, until browned on all sides, then transfer to a baking sheet.

To make the sauce, add a little oil to the same skillet, if needed, and the onion. Cook the onion over medium heat for about 15 minutes, until lightly browned. Stir in the tomato paste, dill, cinnamon, turmeric, and water. Bring to a boil, then lower the heat to a simmer and season to taste with salt and pepper. Delicately place the meatballs in the sauce. Cover and simmer gently for 30 minutes, until the meatballs are cooked through. Stir in the lemon juice and serve warm.

Vegetarian Option

Use an equivalent amount of tempeh in place of the meat, and pulse it in a food processor until coarsely ground. Use 3 eggs instead of 2 eggs.

parvin's tamarind stuffed fish

This tart baked trout is inspired by my cousin Parvin's Norooz fish recipe, and its easy, quick preparation is good news for anyone who's ever been anxious about cooking a whole fish. Trout is reasonably priced, often deboned and therefore easy to eat, and among the very fastest-cooking fish. Try coarsely chopped cranberries or tart cherries if you can't find barberries. You can make the filling a day ahead, but stuff the fish just before baking.

serves 4

4 farmed rainbow or brook trout, 8 ounces each, cleaned and butterflied
Sea salt and freshly ground black pepper
5 tablespoons grapeseed oil
1 large yellow onion, thinly sliced
3 cloves garlic, minced

1 cup whole raw almonds, coarsely ground
1 cup barberries, soaked in warm water for 1/2 hour and drained
1/4 cup Thai tamarind concentrate (see page 16), strained to remove grit

1 cup tightly packed minced fresh herbs, any combination of at least two of the following: cilantro, flat-leaf parsley, tarragon, basil, mint
2 limes, cut into wedges

Preheat the oven to 375°F. Grease two baking sheets.

Rinse the fish under cold water and pat dry thoroughly. Season them inside and out with salt and pepper and divide them between the baking sheets. Set aside in the refrigerator.

Heat a large skillet over medium-high heat. Add 3 tablespoons of the oil and sauté the onion for 10 minutes, until it starts to darken, then cook slowly over low heat for about 30 minutes, until it is dark brown and about half its original volume. Add the garlic, almonds, barberries, and tamarind, and cook over low heat until the mixture becomes fragrant, about 10 minutes. Stir in the herbs and season with salt and pepper. Let cool to room temperature.

Remove the fish from the refrigerator. Open each fish toward you, leaving the bottom flat against the pan. Spread the filling evenly from head to tail, then press the top half of the fish down firmly to cover the filling. Tuck any excess filling inside. Brush the fish with the remaining 2 tablespoons oil.

Bake for 12 to 15 minutes, until the top turns golden and the fish flakes easily. Serve with the lime wedges.

Celebrating the Seasons: Persian Holidays and Iran's Zoroastrian Legacy

Taking the first footstep with a good thought the second with a good word and the third with a good deed I entered Paradise.

—Zarathustra

Iran has been a Muslim country for many centuries, but before the Islamic conquest in the seventh century CE, the Persian Empire was Zoroastrian. The tenets of this little-known but extremely influential religion are said to have been revealed to the prophet Zoroaster (or Zarathustra) around 1200 BCE. Zoroaster, adherents believe, experienced a great vision that told him to worship the one benevolent god Ahura Mazda, the "creator of everything good."

A departure for Iran's pagan society, this curious new religion would introduce several novel ideas to the world, including direct contact with the divine, equality between the genders, and kindness to animals. Prefacing the Judeo-Christian tradition, Zoroastrianism teaches that life is ruled by dualism, resulting in an ongoing conflict in the universe between light and darkness. Within each human being, the faith suggests, there is the free will to choose evil or righteousness, and it's up to the individual to choose "good thoughts, good words, and good deeds" in order to stay on the right path.

The Persian Empire remained Zoroastrian for roughly twelve hundred years, but with the Arab conquest, the majority of Iranians eventually embraced the Islamic faith. Still, many Persians, intent on resisting conversion, fled to India, where their descendants, the Parsis, still practice Zoroastrianism today. In fact, there are an estimated forty-five thousand practicing Zoroastrians in Iran itself, while smaller Zoroastrian communities flourish around the world, including roughly ten thousand in the United States. Despite these diminished numbers, Zoroastrian customs, mythology, and attitudes strongly pervade the Persian cultural identity inside and outside Iran.

A New Day

Spring is here, friends.
Let's stay in the garden
And be guests to the strangers of the green.

We'll fly from one flower to the other,
Like bees making the six corners
Of this earth's hives prosperous.

—Rumi, *Divan-i Kebir*—Meter 1, translated by Nevit O. Ergin

Iran's Zoroastrian roots are perhaps most telling during the winter and summer solstices and the fall and spring equinoxes. Once marked by religious observances, these seasonal milestones have evolved into days of national pride and celebration. The most significant of these events is the Persian New Year celebration *Norooz* (new day), which takes place in March on the spring equinox, when the sun crosses the celestial equator and makes night and day equal again for the first time since the fall equinox on September 21.

This cosmic event, akin to the Christian Easter celebration, marks the beginning of the Iranian New Year, a joyful time of cultural unity that's observed by Persians in and outside of Iran. (Today, *Norooz* often carries a wistful undercurrent, as many expatriate Persians, forced to leave Iran in the years since the 1979 revolution, spend the holiday separated from family and friends.)

In keeping with the *Norooz* spirit of renewal, it's customary for Persians to clean the house, get rid of clutter, buy new clothes, and settle disagreements. A ceremonial table called a *sofreh* is spread with symbolic items, including flowers, candles, a mirror, a goldfish in a bowl, eggs, an orange, and gold coins—all Zoroastrian symbols of hope and prosperity. (You can read more about *sofrehs* and the New Year table on page 152.)

Norooz celebrations are notable for a profusion of green hues, echoing the holiday's emphasis on the reawakening of nature. Even the food at *Norooz* gets the green herb treatment: the classic dinner menu consists of Bean, Herb and Noodle Soup (page 53); as well as fish cooked with herbs, such as Parvin's Tamarind Stuffed Fish (page 90), herbed rice; herb frittata (page 71); and *Sabzi Khordan* (page 27).

Dawn Over Persia

AWAKE! for Morning in the Bowl of Night
Has flung the Stone that puts the Stars
*   to Flight:*
And Lo! the Hunter of the East has caught
The Sultan's Turret in a Noose of Light.

—Omar Khayyam, *The Rubaiyat*, translated by Edward FitzGerald, Dave Gross

The holiday *Shab-e Yalda*, on December 21 (the winter solstice), marks the longest night of the year. For Persians, it represents the victory of light over darkness, as the days only grow longer, and the nights shorter, for the next six months.

Shab-e Yalda, like its sister holiday, Christmas, is a festive occasion, an excuse to stay up past midnight telling jokes, snacking, and reading poetry. *Shab-e Yalda* parties typically include the game *Fal-e-Hafez*, or "Ask Hafez"—one presents a question or concern to the spirit of Persia's legendary poet, and then opens a book of Hafez poetry at random, taking the words as a serendipitous solution to one's question.

Because celebrants are up so late, there are plenty of snacks to keep energy high and hunger at bay throughout the night; this continuous nocturnal snacking is known as *chap charee*, or "night grazing." Traditional dishes for this winter celebration include Eggplant and Tomato Stew with Pomegranate Molasses (page 107) Saffron Rice (page 123), Turmeric Chicken with Sumac and Lime (page 103), and yogurt.

Harvest Moon

Mehregan is the celebration of the autumnal equinox, when the sun crosses the celestial equator moving northward on October 9 or 10. This holiday commemorates the beginning of the world when Ahura Mazda destroyed evil with the help of the goddess Mehr, a deity of love whose power was so strong that she turned the world upside down and defeated the Devil in the process.

This ancient harvest festival honors love and generosity, and it's become customary in Iran to make a *ash-e khirat*, a "charity soup," to be shared with neighbors and those in need, which is comprised of beans, meat, rice, and herbs. For those with a sweet tooth, seven different kinds of Persian pastries are served, as well.

The Rain Festival

Imagine a holiday that's essentially a national waterfight, when you can expect to be drenched by a bucket of water, or find yourself frolicking in a fountain. That's *Tirgan*, or The Rain Festival, celebrated on July 1, just after the summer solstice. It's meant to summon down rains when Iran is at its hottest and pay homage to the divine water that keeps crops and people alive.

The foods served on *Tirgan* can include *shooly*, a soup of spinach and beets, and *sholeh zard*, a rice pudding flavored with rose water (page 157).

olive oil–poached fish with fresh herbs and lemon

This summery dish is inspired by the cuisine of Turkey, which strikes a sophisticated balance between the food of its European and Middle Eastern neighbors. Poaching is a wonderful way to cook with olive oil, because the low heat used in poaching leaves the delicate nature of the oil intact. You'll want to adjust the heat from time to time, as the flame has to be both powerful enough to cook the fish and low enough that it doesn't burn the garlic. Serve with a crisp white wine and warm flatbread to soak up the pan juice.

serves 4

1¹/₂ pounds US-caught swordfish fillet or other meaty white fish like Pacific halibut or Atlantic cod, cut into 1¹/₂-inch pieces
Sea salt and freshly ground black pepper

¹/₂ cup extra-virgin olive oil
3 cloves garlic, minced
Zest of 1 lemon
5 tablespoons freshly squeezed lemon juice

2 cups loosely packed fresh dill, minced
2 cups loosely packed fresh flat-leaf parsley, minced

Season the fish with 1 teaspoon salt and 1 teaspoon pepper.

Heat the oil in a large, deep pan over low heat for 1 minute. Stir in the garlic and lemon zest, then place the fish in the pan in a single layer and cook for 5 minutes undisturbed. Turn the fish and cook for 5 minutes, or until it's just opaque in the center. Turn off the heat and add the lemon juice. Fold in the herbs and season with salt and pepper.

Let the fish rest for 5 minutes before serving, or let cool completely and serve at room temperature. The fish tastes best within a day of being made.

Vegetarian Option

Replace the fish with an equivalent amount of meaty mushrooms such as portobellos, morels, or hen-of-the-woods (maitake), or simply use button mushrooms, sliced in half. Increase the poaching time to 20 minutes, and taste the mushrooms for doneness before taking them off the heat, because you may want to cook them a little longer.

lamb kebabs in pomegranate-walnut marinade

kebab-e torsh

This sweet-and-sour kebab is from Gilan Province in northern Iran, where people like their food extra tart. The russet-colored marinade uses the same ingredients as Fesenjan (Pomegranate Walnut Stew, page 109), and is one of the tastiest discoveries I made while researching this book. Before grilling the kebabs, brush off the extra marinade, because it can burn and leave charred flakes on the meat. You can also make these kebabs using beef sirloin, fish, chicken, or vegetables. Start this recipe the day before you plan to serve it so that the kebabs can marinate overnight.

serves 6

2 pounds lamb tenderloin or
    boneless shank or neck, cut
    into 1¹/₂-inch chunks
1 cup walnuts
³/₄ cup pomegranate molasses

2 cloves garlic, crushed
2 tablespoons grapeseed oil
1 cup loosely packed fresh
    flat-leaf parsley, plus extra
    chopped for garnish

Sea salt and freshly ground black
    pepper

Place the meat in a large casserole dish. In a food processor, grind the walnuts, pomegranate molasses, garlic, and olive oil into a puree. Add the parsley and pulse into small bits. Pour the marinade over the meat and toss well. Cover and refrigerate overnight.

If using wooden or bamboo skewers, soak them in salty water for a couple of hours before grilling. Thread 3 or 4 pieces of meat onto each skewer ¹/₄ inch apart, leaving 2 inches of space at the end. Discard the marinade. Brush or wipe extra marinade from the skewers. Leave the meat out while you heat the grill so it can come up to room temperature (no more than 45 minutes total).

Prepare a hot grill.

Lightly oil the grill and grill the kebabs for 6 to 8 minutes, turning occasionally. When done, the meat should be slightly charred on the outside and very pink on the inside.

continued

Transfer to a serving platter and season with salt and pepper. Garnish with parsley and serve.

Vegetarian Option

Replace the lamb with 2 pounds tempeh, cubed; 2 pounds vegetables, such as zucchini, red onions, and mushrooms, cubed; or a combination of tempeh and vegetables. Marinate overnight according to the recipe.

grilled liver with cumin, garlic, and fresh basil

I sampled grilled lamb's liver for the first time at a Persian cafeteria in Orange County, California, at the urging of my cousin Iraj, who sold me on it by trumpeting its status as a beloved Iranian street food. With great reluctance, I took a bite and was astonished to find that I suddenly liked liver. The cumin in this marinade gives the liver a smoky richness, and the basil brightens its earthy taste. Marinate the liver overnight to give it time to absorb the flavors. It may be difficult to find lamb liver, so feel free to use chicken liver in its place and use skewers to place it on the grill. Make sure that the meat is very fresh, and avoid overcooking, which can give the liver a rubbery texture. The meat should still be a little pink inside when done. If you don't have a grill, sear the liver in a pan.

serves 4

2 teaspoons cumin seeds
2 cloves garlic, minced
1 tablespoon extra-virgin olive oil, plus extra for finishing

Sea salt and freshly ground black pepper
8 ounces lamb or chicken liver
Flatbread

1 bunch basil
1 juicy lemon, quartered

Toast the cumin seeds in a dry skillet over medium heat for about 2 minutes, until they start to release their scent. Transfer to a plate and let cool, then grind into powder.

In a medium bowl, whisk the cumin with the garlic, olive oil, 1 teaspoon salt, and a few grinds of pepper. Add the liver and stir to coat. Cover and marinate in the refrigerator overnight.

Prepare a hot grill.

Lightly oil the grill and grill the liver for 3 to 4 minutes per side, until the meat is just pink on the inside. Cut the liver into a few pieces.

Stuff a piece of bread with several basil leaves and a few pieces of warm liver. Season with lemon juice, olive oil, salt, and pepper.

Vegetarian Option

Use 8 ounces portobello mushrooms, quartered, in place of the liver and marinate overnight.

whole roasted fish with oranges and saffron

In the marinade for this dish, the mix of different citrus juices mimics the flavor of sour oranges, a favorite ingredient in Persian cooking. Meyer lemons are ideal for this purpose, and you'll find them in season from November through March. Use a mandoline to cut the thin orange slices that cover the fish. If they're too thick, they won't bend or drape over the fish easily. Be sure to eat the roasted oranges, too; they're delicious!

serves 4

1 tablespoon grated Meyer
    lemon zest
1/4 cup plus 2 tablespoons freshly
    squeezed Meyer lemon juice
1/4 cup plus 2 tablespoons freshly
    squeezed orange juice
1/2 cup plus 2 tablespoons freshly
    squeezed lime juice

1 (2-pound) red snapper, cod,
    haddock, or sea bass, cleaned
    and butterflied
Sea salt and freshly ground black
    pepper
3 tablespoons grapeseed oil
3 cloves garlic, minced
3 small oranges, for slicing

1/2 teaspoon saffron, ground and
    steeped in 1 tablespoon hot
    water (see page 15)
2 tablespoons extra-virgin
    olive oil

Preheat the oven to 400°F. Oil a baking sheet with grapeseed oil.

In a bowl, whisk the lemon zest and juice with the orange juice and lime juice.

Rub the fish inside and out with salt and pepper and 2 tablespoons of the grapeseed oil. Spread the garlic on the inside of the fish. Slice the oranges on a mandoline as thinly as possible, less than 1/8 inch thick. Open the fish and lay a few orange slices inside (this is a good place for imperfect slices), then press the fish closed. With a sharp knife, make several shallow slits in the top of the fish, without completely slicing through. Drizzle a few tablespoons of the citrus juice over the fish, and cover it from head to tail with the rest of the orange slices. Spoon the remaining 1 tablespoon grapeseed oil on top, and season with salt.

Bake for about 35 minutes, until the fish flakes easily with a fork. Heat the citrus juice in a small skillet over medium-high heat until bubbling and reduce by half. Turn off the heat and whisk in the saffron and extra-virgin olive oil. Serve the fish warm, topped with the citrus sauce.

chicken kebabs in yogurt marinade

joojeh kebab

When you bite into hot joojeh—recognizable from a distance by its saffron-orange and charcoal-black markings—your teeth break through a charred and steaming exterior to meat that's moist and flavorful. The trick to making good joojeh is to marinate it overnight in a tenderizing mixture of lemon, yogurt, and garlic. You can use this recipe to make excellent baked chicken, too (see Variation below).

serves 6

6 cloves garlic, minced
³/₄ cup freshly squeezed lemon
   juice
1 cup plain yogurt (not thick)
1 teaspoon ground turmeric
Sea salt and freshly ground black
   pepper

2 pounds boneless, skinless
   chicken breasts, cut into
   1-inch pieces
1 pint cherry tomatoes
¹/₄ cup extra-virgin olive oil

¹/₂ teaspoon saffron, ground and
   steeped in 2 teaspoons hot
   water (see page 15)
Sumac, for garnish

In a large bowl, whisk the garlic with ¹/₂ cup of the lemon juice, the yogurt, and the turmeric. Taste and season with 2 teaspoons salt and 1 teaspoon pepper. Fold in the chicken, coating evenly. Cover and refrigerate for up to 24 hours.

If using wooden or bamboo skewers, soak them in salty water for a couple of hours before grilling. Drain the chicken and shake off the extra marinade. Thread the chicken onto the skewers about ¹/₄ inch apart, along with a few tomatoes on each skewer, leaving 2 inches of space at the end. Dust with salt and pepper.

Prepare a hot grill.

Whisk the remaining ¹/₄ cup lemon juice with the olive oil and saffron and brush it on the chicken. Grill the chicken, turning it frequently and basting often with the saffron mixture for about 15 minutes, until the meat is lightly charred on the outside and just cooked through. Season with salt and pepper, garnish with sumac, and serve.

To bake the chicken, cut each breast into three or four pieces and marinate overnight according to the recipe, then shake off the marinade and brown the chicken in a skillet. Cover and bake at 350°F for 20 minutes, until cooked through. Spoon the basting sauce on top to serve.

Replace the chicken with 2 pounds tempeh, cubed; 2 pounds vegetables, such as zucchini, red onions, and mushrooms, cubed; or a combination of tempeh and vegetables. Marinate overnight according to the recipe.

What Is Halal Food?

Halal translates as "permissible" in Arabic, and it refers to the dietary laws of Muslims as they are recorded in the Koran. Much like the kosher laws followed by observant Jews, halal guidelines are quite specific about how food is sourced or produced. For example, according to a strict interpretation of halal, all meat products must come from an herbivorous animal, which must be slaughtered by a Muslim—indeed, the name of Allah must be mentioned before or during slaughter. Halal also specifies that the animal must be killed humanely, which includes that the animal be alive and healthy at the time of slaughter, that its throat be cut by a razor-sharp knife in a single swipe to cause as little pain as possible, and that the knife must not be sharpened in front of the animal so as to avoid causing it stress. Many Muslims, especially in the United States and other Western countries, follow more liberal interpretations of Halal, and routinely buy non-halal meat at the local supermarket, a practice that's accepted by a number of eminent Muslim scholars. Like Jews, Muslims are forbidden to eat pork. Along with alcohol and intoxicants, pork is haram, or unlawful.

turmeric chicken with sumac and lime

Simple and quick to prepare, this weeknight chicken recipe still boasts all the exotic flavor of more elaborate Persian dishes. I recommend using chicken thighs, which are moister, more flavorful, and cheaper than breasts, and their dark meat contains minerals that you won't find in white meat. Drumsticks and breasts will work just fine here, too, although breasts may require a little more time on the stove because of their density. If you use skinless chicken, increase the amount of cooking oil by a tablespoon or two. Serve the chicken with a fluffy grain, such as rice, millet, or quinoa.

serves 4

1 teaspoon ground turmeric
Sea salt and freshly ground black
    pepper

4 bone-in chicken thighs
2 tablespoons grapeseed oil
$3/4$ cup water

4 cloves garlic, minced
2 juicy limes, halved
Sumac, for garnish

In a small bowl, mix the turmeric with 1 tablespoon salt and 2 teaspoons pepper. Place the chicken on a rimmed baking sheet and sprinkle with the spice mixture, turning to coat both sides.

Heat a large skillet over medium-high heat and add the oil. Brown the chicken well on both sides, about 7 minutes per side. Pour in the water, then add the garlic, stirring it into the water. Bring the water to a boil, then turn down the heat to low and cover. Braise the chicken for 25 minutes, until the inside is opaque. Transfer the chicken to a serving platter, turn up the heat to high, and reduce the cooking liquid for a few minutes, stirring occasionally until it's slightly thickened. Season to taste with salt and pepper, and pour the sauce over the chicken.

Dust the chicken with sumac and pepper, garnish with lime halves, and serve.

Vegetarian Option

Use whole portobello mushrooms in place of the chicken, or use 1 pound firm tofu, well drained and cut into slabs 1 inch thick. You will need a little extra oil for searing than what is called for in the recipe.

main dish stews and casseroles

Persian stew, or *khoresh*, is the crowning glory of Persian cuisine, a culinary pageant in which the fruits and vegetables of a biblical land show off their bright colors and flavors, from sour to sweet, spicy to savory. The recipes in this chapter offer just a sample of the ingredients likely to find their way into a Persian stew, including eggplants, tomatoes, peaches, green herbs, dried limes, rhubarb, tamarind, split peas, kidney beans, and barley.

In exotic pairings like pomegranate with chicken, fish with tamarind, and lamb with rhubarb, you find the trademark combination of fruit and meat in Persian cooking. These bedazzled dishes have been around since the Greeks began writing about the food of their archrivals some five hundred years before Christ. Even then, it was likely understood by the Persians that the acid in fruit cuts through animal fat, making it tastier and more digestible. There's ample evidence that the pairing of fruit and meat spread from Persia throughout the Arab world and into Europe via trade routes, invasions, and the Crusades, inspiring such iconic Western dishes as duck à l'orange, mincemeat pie (originally made with meat and fruit), and even American turkey with cranberry sauce.

To better understand why Persian stews are so renowned and influential, it helps to understand that they're considerably thicker than Western stews, more like rich casseroles that merit being the center of a meal. Too thick to be a soup, *khoresh* isn't eaten with a spoon but instead is meant to be ladled over fluffy white rice, or another whole grain. The one exception to that rule in this chapter is the recipe for *Kharcho* (Barley Stew with Lamb and Rhubarb, page 111), a delectable version of *khoresh* from a little farther west of Iran, in Georgia—there the grain is cooked right into the stew. Usually, stew and rice are accompanied with tangy yogurt, because it lightens and brightens the whole meal. For kosher eaters, however, extra lime juice, lemon juice, or a condiment of sour pickles can balance the meal in much the same way.

The Persian Gulf specialty *Ghaliyeh Mahi* (Persian Gulf–Style Spicy Tamarind Fish Stew, page 117) shows off India's influence on Iranian cooking in the form of spicy chile peppers, which are virtually unseen in Iran outside of the southern region. The recipe for *Ghormeh Sabzi* (Green Herb and Kidney Bean Stew, page 115), traditionally made with lamb or chicken, is reconfigured here with meaty tofu, for a satisfying and heart-healthy take on a time-honored favorite. Finally, *Fesenjan* (Pomegranate Walnut Stew, page 109) is a stellar example of the magic of *malas*, the Persian term for "sweet and sour." Surely, this dish is what must have charmed the palates of Europeans so many centuries ago.

eggplant and tomato stew with pomegranate molasses

bademjan

Make this rich stew on a lazy day when you have time to caramelize the onions until they're dark and sweet, then cook the stew and let it rest for a while on the stove before eating to let the flavors develop. It's important to use Japanese eggplants in this recipe, because their flesh is sweeter than regular eggplant and they have fewer and smaller seeds. Traditionally, the eggplant is fried before being added to the stew, but in the interest of health, I've chosen to roast it instead, using very little oil, and I'm happy to report that the result is simply delectable. I prefer to use a sweetened pomegranate molasses in this recipe, but if you have the unsweetened variety, you can add a shot of honey to balance the flavors: start with 1 tablespoon and sweeten to taste. You can bake off the eggplant and cook the split peas the day before.

serves 4

2 pounds Japanese eggplant, peeled and diced
Sea salt
5 tablespoons grapeseed oil
1/2 cup split peas
8 cups water

1 yellow onion, thinly sliced
4 medium to large tomatoes (2 pounds), coarsely chopped
1/2 teaspoon ground turmeric
1/2 teaspoon ground cinnamon
1/4 cup pomegranate molasses

3 cloves garlic, minced
4 cups vegetable or chicken stock, boiling
Freshly ground black pepper

Preheat the oven to 425°F. Line a baking sheet with parchment paper.

Spread the eggplant on the prepared baking sheet. Sprinkle with 1 teaspoon salt and 1 tablespoon of the oil. Bake for 40 minutes, stirring gently every 10 minutes to prevent sticking. When the eggplant is completely soft, let it cool to room temperature.

While the eggplant cooks, combine the split peas with the water in a saucepan. Bring to a boil, then turn down the heat and simmer, covered, for about 40 minutes, until the peas are tender. Drain and season with 1 teaspoon salt.

continued

Heat the remaining 4 tablespoons oil in a Dutch oven or a large, deep skillet over medium-high heat. Add the onion and cook for 10 minutes, until it starts to darken, then cook slowly over low heat for about 30 minutes, until it is dark brown and about half its original volume. Add the eggplant, tomatoes, turmeric, cinnamon, pomegranate molasses, garlic, split peas, and 1 teaspoon salt. Add the stock and bring to a boil, then lower the heat and simmer, partially covered, for 1 hour. Uncover and simmer for 15 minutes, until the stew is thick.

Turn off the heat and let the stew rest for 15 to 30 minutes. Season with salt and pepper and serve.

pomegranate walnut stew

fesenjan

The sweet-and-sour flavor of fesenjan, *a classic Iranian stew regularly featured on the menus of weddings and special occasions, is the magical combination of rich ground walnuts and tart pomegranate syrup. Served on a bed of fluffy rice and decorated with jewel-like pomegranate seeds, this stew makes a stunning addition to any holiday table.*

serves 4

Grapeseed oil, for searing
Sea salt
2 pounds skinless chicken legs or breasts
2 yellow onions, finely diced

1 cup walnuts, coarsely ground
$^1/_2$ cup pomegranate molasses
2 cups chicken stock, vegetable stock, or water, hot

1 cup peeled and grated red beets
Pomegranate seeds (see page 62), for garnish

Heat a large, deep skillet over medium-high heat and add 1 tablespoon oil to the pan. Lightly salt the chicken and sear for 6 to 7 minutes per side, until well browned, then transfer to a plate.

In the same skillet, sauté the onions over medium heat for about 15 minutes, until lightly browned.

Add the walnuts, pomegranate molasses, and 2 teaspoons salt, and stir to coat the onions. Add the stock and bring to a boil. Lower the heat to a simmer and return the chicken to the stew. Cover and cook for 25 minutes. Stir in the beets and cook, uncovered, for 15 to 20 minutes, until the stew is thick and the beets are tender. Salt to taste.

Pull out the chicken pieces with tongs and cut them in halves or thirds. Put a few pieces of chicken on each plate, along with plenty of sauce. Garnish with the pomegranate seeds, and serve.

Vegetarian Option

Substitute two 8-ounce packages tempeh, halved, for the chicken, and sear in 3 tablespoons of oil for 3 to 4 minutes per side. Cook the onions in 2 to 3 tablespoons oil instead of the chicken fat, and dice the tempeh before serving.

barley stew with lamb and rhubarb

I first tasted this stew at a Russian banya (bathhouse) in Brighton Beach, Brooklyn, after an evening of schvitzing. It hails from Georgia, the former Soviet country on the Black Sea whose cuisine has many similarities to Iranian food. Traditionally this stew gets a blast of flavor from sour plum paste, a specialty of the region, but I chose to substitute rhubarb, taking my inspiration from a classic Persian rhubarb stew. Marinate the lamb overnight, or the meat will be bland. Add the rhubarb at the very end, and stop cooking before the rhubarb falls apart, or the flavor will be lost.

serves 6 as a main course

2 pounds boneless lamb
    shoulder, cut into
    1-inch pieces
Sea salt and freshly ground black
    pepper

MARINADE
$1^1/_2$ cups dry white wine
4 cloves garlic, minced
1 tablespoon allspice
1 tablespoon ground coriander
2 tablespoons tomato paste

STEW
2 yellow onions, thinly sliced
4 tablespoons grapeseed oil
$1^1/_2$ cups dry white wine
4 cloves garlic, minced
1 tablespoon allspice
1 tablespoon ground coriander
2 tablespoons tomato paste
$3/_4$ cup pearled barley
6 cups water
1 pound rhubarb stalks,
    finely diced

$3/_4$ cup freshly squeezed lemon
    juice, for garnish
1 bunch cilantro, flat-leaf parsley,
    or a mix, coarsely chopped,
    for garnish
Red pepper flakes, for garnish

Soak the lamb in cold water for 5 minutes, then drain and dry thoroughly. Place the lamb in a baking dish and season with 2 teaspoons salt and 1 teaspoon pepper. To make the marinade, whisk together the wine, garlic, allspice, coriander, and tomato paste. Pour the marinade over the lamb and cover. Marinate overnight in the refrigerator.

Drain the lamb. In a large stockpot, soften the onions in the oil over medium heat for a few minutes. Increase the heat to medium-high and lightly brown the lamb all over for about 5 minutes. Add the wine, garlic, allspice, coriander, tomato paste, and the barley. Add the water and bring to a boil; then lower the heat and simmer, covered, for about $1^1/_2$ hours, until the barley and lamb are tender.

continued

Add the rhubarb and cook for 15 minutes, until the rhubarb is just soft but the pieces are still intact. Season with salt and pepper. Splash each serving with 2 tablespoons lemon juice, a scattering of herbs, and a pinch of red pepper flakes.

Vegetarian Option

Replace the lamb with diced meaty mushrooms such as portobello, morel, or hen-of-the-woods (maitake), and prepare them the same way as the lamb.

seared chicken with peaches

khoresh-e hulu

Orange-gold peaches are a sweet Silk Road treasure that traveled from China to Iran more than two thousand years ago, and they're seen today in the glittering and fragrant display cases of Persian dried fruit stores. Make this dish in summer when peaches are abundant, or substitute plums or pears in the fall.

serves 6

2 pounds skinless chicken legs
  or breasts
Sea salt and freshly ground black
  pepper
5 tablespoons grapeseed oil
1 yellow onion, diced

1 pound ripe peaches, peeled
  and sliced into 1-inch wedges
1/2 teaspoon ground turmeric
1/2 teaspoon ground cinnamon
1/2 cup freshly squeezed
  lemon juice

2 teaspoons grated lemon zest
1/2 teaspoon saffron, ground and
  steeped in 1 tablespoon hot
  water (see page 15)
2 cups water, simmering

Season the chicken with salt and pepper. Heat a large skillet over medium-high heat and add 3 tablespoons of the oil to the pan. Add the chicken and sear 6 to 7 minutes per side, until well browned, then transfer to a plate.

In the same skillet, cook the onion over medium-high heat in the remaining 2 tablespoons oil for about 10 minutes, just until they start to brown. Add the peaches, turmeric, cinnamon, lemon juice, lemon zest, saffron, and water. Bring to a boil, then lower the heat and return the chicken to the pan. Simmer, partially covered, for 30 minutes; then uncover and simmer for 10 minutes to thicken. Season to taste with salt and pepper.

Pull out the chicken pieces with tongs and cut the boneless pieces in half or in thirds. Put a few pieces of chicken on each plate along with several peach slices and plenty of sauce.

Vegetarian Option

Substitute tempeh or firm tofu for the chicken. If using tofu, drain the tofu and press it under a heavy weight for 1 hour, in order to press out as much water as possible. Before cooking, cut the tofu into slabs 1 inch thick, or cut the tempeh in half to form 2 squares. You may need to use a little more oil for searing the tempeh or tofu. Before serving, cut the tempeh or tofu into thirds.

green herb and kidney bean stew

ghormeh sabzi

This green stew studded with red kidney beans is one of the most famous in Persian cuisine. Although it's usually made with chicken, it works surprisingly well with tofu, which is frozen, thawed, and baked here to give it a meaty texture. Start this recipe the day before you plan to serve it, so the tofu has time to freeze through and then defrost. If you prefer to use chicken, follow the instructions in the Variation below.

serves 4

1 (14-ounce) package firm tofu
5 tablespoons grapeseed oil
Sea salt and freshly ground black
    pepper
1 teaspoon ground turmeric
1 large yellow onion, thinly sliced
4 cloves garlic, minced
2 cups cooked kidney beans
    (one 15-ounce can), rinsed
    and drained

2 cups vegetable or chicken
    stock, boiling
1/2 pound spinach, coarsely
    chopped
1 cup tightly packed, coarsely
    chopped fresh flat-leaf parsley
1 cup tightly packed, coarsely
    chopped fresh cilantro

1 cup thinly sliced scallions
2 dried limes, soaked in hot
    water to cover for 15 minutes
3 tablespoons freshly squeezed
    lemon juice
Extra-virgin olive oil, for finishing

Drain the tofu and cut it into 1-inch-thick slabs. Freeze until solid, about 6 hours, then defrost in the refrigerator overnight. Squeeze the tofu slices to remove excess water.

Preheat the oven to 375°F. Line a baking sheet with a nonstick baking mat.

In a medium bowl, whisk together 2 tablespoons of the grapeseed oil, 1 teaspoon salt, a few grinds of pepper, and the turmeric. Add the tofu and toss to coat it in the seasoning. Spread the tofu on the baking sheet and bake for 50 minutes, flipping the slabs once halfway through. The tofu should be golden and springy. Let cool and dice.

While the tofu bakes, caramelize the onion. Heat a large, deep skillet over medium-high heat and add the remaining 3 tablespoons grapeseed oil, followed by the onion. Brown the onion for 10 minutes, until it starts to darken, then cook slowly over low heat for

continued

about 30 minutes, until it is dark brown and about half its original volume. Add the garlic, beans, tofu, and stock and bring to a boil; then turn down the heat and simmer, partially covered, for 30 minutes.

Add the spinach in large handfuls, adding more as each batch wilts, then stir in the herbs and scallions. Pierce the limes and add them to the stew along with their soaking water. Simmer for 20 minutes. The herbs should be tender but still bright green. Stir in the lemon juice and season with salt and pepper. Turn off the heat and let the stew rest for 15 minutes. Drizzle with extra-virgin olive oil and serve.

Variation

Heat a large, deep skillet over medium-high heat and add 1 tablespoon grapeseed oil to the pan. Lightly salt 2 pounds skinless chicken breasts and legs. Add the chicken to the skillet and sear for 6 to 7 minutes per side, until well browned, then transfer to a plate. Add the chicken to the stew along with the beans.

persian gulf–style spicy tamarind fish stew

ghaliyeh mahi

If you think this hot, tangy fish with cilantro resembles something you might eat in Mexico, you have the right idea. Though tamarind plays a significant role in Mexican food, it originally hails from across the globe in Africa—that's how far and wide global cuisine has traveled! If you don't like cilantro, you can substitute a combination of parsley and mint instead. I recommend using serrano chiles, but Anaheims or jalapeños will taste terrific, too.

serves 4

1¹/₂ pounds firm, white-fleshed skinless fish fillet, such as Atlantic cod, Pacific halibut, or US-caught swordfish
2 yellow onions, diced
¹/₄ cup refined coconut oil

4 cloves garlic, minced
1 teaspoon ground turmeric
2 cups Thai tamarind concentrate (see page 16), strained to remove grit

3 red or green serrano chiles, seeded and thinly sliced
Sea salt
About 2 cups tightly packed fresh cilantro, coarsely chopped

Wash the fish, dry thoroughly, and cut it into 1¹/₂-inch pieces.

In a large skillet, sauté the onions in the oil over medium heat for about 15 minutes, until lightly browned. Add the garlic, turmeric, tamarind, 1 of the chiles, and 1 teaspoon salt, and let the mixture bubble gently for a few minutes. Add the fish and simmer, uncovered, for 20 minutes, until the fish is just cooked through. Stir often.

Fold in the cilantro and add salt to taste. Garnish with a few chile slices and serve the rest on the side.

Vegetarian Option

Substitute firm tofu for the fish. Before cooking, drain the tofu and press it under a heavy weight for 1 hour, to press out as much water as possible.

rice and grains

For Persians, the preparation of rice is an art form, and virtually every Persian meal comes with a perfect pillowy mound of pilaf. Rice makes a fluffy bed for the rich stews and kebabs that Iran is known for, but with the addition of meat, fruit, nuts, beans, and herbs, rice can be an entrée in itself. Rice arrived in Persia from the East, where India and China had already been cultivating it for thousands of years. In time, this versatile grain came to rival wheat bread as the main starch in the Iranian diet.

In general, Persians favor long-grain rice. Here in the States, basmati rice imported from India is an excellent choice for making Persian-style rice dishes. Persians have time-tested ways of preparing their favorite grain, and the most elegant—and admittedly complex—way is to parboil the rice, and then steam it (see page 128). This two-step process produces rice that's lighter and fluffier than rice that's cooked only once. Still, these recipes all work beautifully with rice that's cooked according to standard methods. In this chapter, you'll find instructions for both simple and more advanced techniques.

Any of these rice recipes can be made using a whole grain like quinoa, millet, or barley (see page 19). In fact, some dishes in the following pages call for whole grains instead of rice in order to illustrate just how well this substitution works.

jeweled brown basmati rice and quinoa

morassa polo

This dish gets its name from the gemlike red barberries and green pistachios that sparkle on its surface. It's a regal dish that's typically reserved for special occasions. My husband and I served jeweled rice at our wedding, and it was so well received that the wedding venue added it to their menu. Although there are quite a few ingredients, this is an easy dish to make. You simply sauté the dried fruit and nuts with oil and spices, and toss them with the cooked grains. If you're substituting different grains for the ones used here, check to see if they need more or less cooking water than the recipe calls for, and adjust accordingly.

serves 6 to 8

1 cup brown basmati rice, soaked in cold water for 1 hour
1 1/2 cups quinoa, soaked in cold water for 1 hour
5 tablespoons grapeseed oil
Sea salt
4 cups water, boiling
2 tablespoons butter or unrefined coconut oil, at room temperature
1 large yellow onion, minced

1/2 cup barberries, soaked in warm water for 1/2 hour and drained
1 cup minced dried apricots
1 tablespoon dried rose petals or dried whole rosebuds pulled apart and stems removed, plus extra for garnish
1 teaspoon ground cumin
1/2 teaspoon ground cinnamon
1 teaspoon ground cardamom

1/2 cup pistachios, lightly toasted and coarsely chopped
1/2 cup slivered blanched almonds, lightly toasted
1/2 teaspoon saffron, ground and steeped in 1 tablespoon hot water (see page 15)
Pomegranate seeds, for garnish (optional)

Drain the rice and quinoa and rinse under cold water. (Try making *tahdig*! Bring a large pot three-quarters full of salted water to a boil, and follow the instructions starting on page 128 for making one of four styles of *tahdig*. Rejoin this recipe in the next to last paragraph, and mix the dried fruit, nuts, rose petals, and spices with the rice and quinoa just as if you've been following this recipe all along. Good luck!)

Heat a medium stockpot over low heat and add the rice and quinoa, 2 tablespoons of the oil, and a pinch of salt. Sauté the grains, stirring often to prevent sticking for about 5 minutes until dry and fragrant. Add the boiling water and return to a boil; turn down the heat

continued

to very low and cook, covered, for 40 minutes. Turn off the heat and let the grains rest for 10 minutes, then toss in the butter and fluff with a fork.

While the grains cook, heat a large skillet over medium heat and sauté the onion in the remaining 3 tablespoons oil for about 15 minutes, until lightly browned. Add the barberries, apricots, rose petals, cumin, cinnamon, and cardamom. Cook for about 5 minutes, until heated through. Reserve half of the pistachios and almonds for garnish, and add the rest of the nuts to the skillet. Season with salt, and remove from the heat.

In a large bowl, toss the fruit and nuts with the grains and drizzle in the saffron. Season with salt. Garnish with the remaining nuts, a few rose petals, and the pomegranate seeds.

saffron rice

chelo

Simple saffron rice is as close to perfection as food can get. It's the classic accompaniment to kebabs, and the basic building block of the towering citadels of fruit-and-nut-studded rice popular at fancy Persian events. Follow this recipe for a basic rice side dish, or consult my guide to making tahdig *to create a crunchy and delicious golden crust. As rice cooking times may vary depending on the variety, check the rice after 15 minutes. For a subtle flavor variation, try using unrefined coconut oil to give the rice a mild coconut aroma that's evocative of India and Thailand. (See photo on page 94.)*

serves 6 to 8

2 cups white basmati rice
3 cups water
1/4 teaspoon sea salt

2 tablespoons butter or unrefined
    coconut oil, at room
    temperature

1/2 teaspoon saffron, ground and
    steeped in 1 tablespoon hot
    water (see page 15)

Soak the rice in cold water for 30 minutes. Drain the rice and rinse under cold water until it runs clear. (Try making *tahdig*! Bring a large pot three-quarters full of salted water to a boil, and follow the instructions on page 128 for making one of four styles of *tahdig*. You'll rejoin this recipe in the final paragraph. Good luck!)

In a stockpot, combine the water and salt and bring to a boil. Add the rice, return to a boil, then turn down the heat to its lowest setting. Cover and cook for 20 minutes. Turn off the heat and let the rice rest for 5 minutes, then dot with the butter and fluff with a fork. The rice should be dry and fluffy. If there's rice stuck to the bottom of the pot, scrape it out and eat it; it's tasty!

Gently scoop all but about 1 cup of the rice onto a serving platter. Toss the reserved rice with the saffron water. Spoon the saffron rice over the white rice as a garnish, and serve.

sweet rice with carrots and nuts

shirin polo

This colorful rice dish infused with orange and cardamom is a close cousin of jeweled rice (page 121); it's a bit less complex but just as beautiful. Traditionally, shirin polo is paired with spiced baked chicken, so you may want to prepare it with the Turmeric Chicken with Sumac and Lime (page 103) or the Chicken Kebabs in Yogurt Marinade (page 100). Be sure to zest only the outer layer of the orange, because the white pith underneath will make the dish bitter. The mild flavor of unrefined coconut oil complements the sweetness of this rice and can make for an interesting variation on the traditional butter.

serves 6 to 8

2 cups white basmati rice, soaked in cold water for 1 hour
3 cups water
Sea salt
2 tablespoons butter or unrefined coconut oil, at room temperature
3 tablespoons unrefined coconut oil

1 yellow onion, finely diced
2 scant cups grated carrots (about 3 large carrots)
$^1/_2$ cup slivered or coarsely chopped almonds, toasted
1 teaspoon ground cinnamon
1 teaspoon ground cardamom
$^1/_4$ teaspoon ground turmeric

$^1/_2$ cup pistachios, coarsely chopped, plus 1 tablespoon for garnish
Grated zest of 1 large orange
$^1/_4$ cup honey
$^1/_2$ teaspoon saffron, ground and steeped in 1 tablespoon hot water (see page 15)

Drain the rice and rinse under cold water until the water runs clear. (Try making *tahdig*! Bring a large pot three-quarters full of salted water to a boil and follow the instructions on page 128 for making one of four styles of *tahdig*. You'll rejoin this recipe in the next to last paragraph, and mix the carrots and nuts with the rice just as if you've been following this recipe all along. Good luck!)

In a stockpot, combine the water and a pinch of salt and bring to a boil. Add the rice, return to a boil, then turn down the heat to its lowest setting. Cover and cook for 20 minutes. Turn off the heat and let the rice rest for 5 minutes, then dot with the butter and fluff with a fork. The rice should be dry and fluffy.

continued

While the rice cooks, heat a small skillet over medium heat and sauté the onion in the coconut oil for about 15 minutes, until lightly browned. Add the carrots, almonds, cinnamon, cardamom, and turmeric, and cook, stirring often, for about 10 minutes, until the carrots are tender. Add 1/2 cup pistachios, the orange zest, and the honey and cook for about 2 minutes, until heated through. Season with salt.

Scoop the rice into a large bowl. Add the carrot mixture and drizzle in the saffron. Mix gently and season with salt. Garnish with the remaining 1 tablespoon pistachios.

rice with rose petals and barberries

zereshk polo

This rice is like a garden, filled with fragrant rose petals and brilliant berries, but its sweet appearance belies a deep, savory taste that's punctuated by bold bursts of tartness. This is my simplified version of barberry rice, a classic Persian dish that's far more complex than this one. If you can't find barberries, substitute coarsely chopped dried cranberries or dried sour cherries.

serves 6 to 8

2 cups white basmati rice, soaked
    in cold water for 1 hour
3 cups water
Sea salt
2 tablespoons butter or
    unrefined coconut oil,
    at room temperature

2 shallots, minced
3 tablespoons grapeseed oil
$^1/_4$ cup dried rose petals or dried
    whole rosebuds pulled apart
    and stems removed, plus
    extra for garnish

$^1/_2$ cup barberries, soaked in
    warm water for $^1/_2$ hour and
    drained
$^1/_2$ teaspoon saffron, ground and
    steeped in 1 tablespoon hot
    water (see page 15)

Drain the rice and rinse under cold water until the water runs clear. (Try making *tahdig*! Bring a large pot three-quarters full of salted water to a boil, and follow the instructions on page 128 for making one of four styles of *tahdig*. You'll rejoin this recipe in the next to last paragraph, and mix the rose petals and barberries with the rice just as if you've been following this recipe all along. Good luck!)

In a stockpot, bring the water to a boil with a pinch of salt. Add the rice, return to a boil, then turn down the heat to its lowest setting. Cover and cook for 20 minutes. Turn off the heat and let the rice rest for 5 minutes, then dot with the butter and fluff with a fork. The rice should be dry and fluffy.

While the rice cooks, heat a small sauté pan over medium heat and sauté the shallots in the oil for about 10 minutes, until they just start to brown. Add the rose petals and barberries and cook, stirring often, for 10 minutes, until the barberries are tender.

In a large bowl, combine the barberry mixture with the rice and drizzle the saffron over the top. Mix gently and season to taste with salt. Garnish with rose petals.

How to Make Tahdig

If you like crackly pan scraps, have an appetite for anything extra crispy, or if you prefer your food more darkly tanned than pale, then you must try making *tahdig* (pronounced *tah-DEEG*). Tahdig is the panfried layer of crust at the bottom of the rice pot and, in fact, it literally translates as "the bottom of the pot" in Persian. When made well, *tahdig* looks like a perfectly caramelized disk, and it can be detached from the pot and served whole, or broken into jagged, golden shards. At Iranian family feasts, *tahdig* is possibly the one dish that will disappear entirely from the table—there are simply no leftovers. Ever. Think of *tahdig* as Persian "soul food." It's the ultimate in crunchy, golden goodness—somewhere between fried chicken and popcorn—and making it is a skill worth perfecting. (See the *tahdig* layer on top of the *tah chin* on page 138.)

The basic premise of making *tahdig* is that by putting extra cooking fat in the bottom of the rice pot (or skillet, which is what I use), the bottom layer of the rice gets panfried while the rice above it gets steamed. There are a handful of classic approaches to making *tahdig*. The simplest is to use plain rice. Another method is to mix the rice with yogurt to give it a thick, pasty texture before spreading it in the pot. Yet another technique is to line the bottom of the pot with a layer of flat lavash bread before topping it with rice.

Both the yogurt and bread methods help ensure that the *tahdig* comes out intact—they are tricks to help the cook, if you will. The final and perhaps most glorious method of making *tahdig* calls for adding sliced potatoes to the bottom of the pan. This last is pure embellishment, with no purpose other than making the *tahdig* even tastier.

Below are instructions for how to make each of the four variations that I've described. The rice recipes in this book are written as simple pilafs,

but you can use these techniques to give any one of them a layer of *tahdig*.

You can add a dash of color and flavor to *tahdig* by sprinkling it with a pinch of turmeric or a pinch of ground saffron steeped in 1 tablespoon hot water, before layering the rest of the rice on top.

With any of the following *tahdig* methods, you can stir a single whisked egg white into the rice before spreading it over the bottom of the pan. Although it will make your *tahdig* taste mildly of egg, the egg white ensures that your *tahdig* will not fall apart.

Note: To make *tahdig* using a whole grain, simply follow the instructions in Step 1 of the Basic Rice with *Tahdig* recipe (below). Check the grain as it boils to see when it's almost cooked through, as it will take a whole grain longer than white rice to reach the parcooked stage. When the grain is parcooked, drain it under cold water and proceed with Step 2.

Basic Rice with Tahdig

makes 5½ cups rice plus one 10-inch disk of tahdig

2 cups white basmati rice

3 tablespoons refined coconut oil, ghee, or grapeseed oil

¼ teaspoon sea salt

Step 1: Parcook the rice

Soak the rice in cold water for 30 minutes. Swish the rice around a few times, then drain and rinse the rice in cold water until the rinse water runs clear. In a stockpot, combine 8 cups water and 2 heaping tablespoons salt and bring to a boil. Add the rice and return to a boil, uncovered, as it can easily boil over. After 5 minutes, test a grain of the rice by breaking it in half. The rice is ready when it's soft but the center is still opaque and not fully cooked. Drain and rinse the rice under cold water to stop the cooking. Measure out 2 cups rice and set aside.

Step 2: Make the tahdig layer

Heat a deep 10-inch cast-iron skillet or enamel paella pan over low heat for a few minutes. Add the oil (if your skillet is bigger than 10 inches, add an additional 2 tablespoons oil), followed by the 2 cups reserved rice. Spread the rice evenly over the bottom of the pan, and pack it down tightly with an offset spatula or large wooden spoon. Sprinkle the sea salt over the rice.

Step 3: Shape the rice into a pyramid and cook

Add the rest of the rice and shape it into a pyramid. Poke several holes in the rice with a chopstick to let steam escape. Cover and turn the heat up to medium-high. Cook the rice for 10 minutes, then turn down the heat to very low and place a clean dish towel or *damkoni* (see page 133) under the lid to catch condensation, and cover the pan tightly. If you have a flame tamer, put it between the burner and the bottom of the skillet to disperse the cooking heat. Cook for 50 minutes.

Step 4: Separate the rice from the tahdig and serve

Lift the lid from the pan. There will be condensation trapped under the lid, so avoid tilting it over the rice and inadvertently pouring the steam water back in. Gently scoop the rice onto a serving platter, making sure not to disturb the *tahdig* at the bottom. Loosen the sides of the *tahdig* with a butter knife and flip it onto a plate, or remove it from the pan with an offset spatula. Serve whole or broken in pieces.

Rice with Yogurt Tahdig

makes 5^1/$_2$ cups rice plus one 10-inch disk of tahdig

Use thick Greek-style yogurt for making yogurt *tahdig* because regular yogurt is too watery to produce a crisp crust. You can make thick yogurt by draining regular yogurt in a fine-mesh sieve or cheesecloth for 8 to 12 hours in the refrigerator. You'll need to drain about four times the amount of yogurt called for, because the yogurt shrinks as it drains.

2 cups white basmati rice

3 tablespoons thick Greek-style yogurt

3 tablespoons refined coconut oil, ghee, or grapeseed oil

^{1}/$_4$ teaspoon sea salt

Step 1: Parcook the rice

Soak the rice in cold water for 30 minutes. Swish the rice around a few times, then drain and rinse the rice in cold water until it runs clear. In a stockpot, combine 8 cups water and 2 heaping tablespoons salt and bring to a boil. Add the rice and return to a boil, uncovered, as it can easily boil over. After 5 minutes, test a grain of the rice by breaking it in half. The rice is ready when it's soft but the center is still opaque and not fully cooked. Drain and rinse the rice under cold water to stop the cooking. Measure out 2 cups rice, mix with the yogurt to form a thick paste, and set aside.

Step 2: Make the tahdig layer

Heat a deep, 10-inch cast-iron skillet or enamel paella pan over low heat for a few minutes. Add the oil (if your skillet is bigger than 10 inches, add an additional 2 tablespoons oil), followed by the yogurt and rice mixture. Spread the mixture evenly over the bottom of the pan, and pack it down tightly with an offset spatula or large wooden spoon. Sprinkle the sea salt over the rice.

Step 3: Shape the rice into a pyramid and cook

Add the rest of the rice and shape it into a pyramid. Poke several holes in the rice with a chopstick to let steam escape. Cover and turn the heat up to medium-high. Cook the rice for 10 minutes, then turn down the heat to very low and place a clean dish towel or *damkoni* (see page 133) under the lid to catch condensation, and cover the pan tightly. If you have a flame tamer, put it between the burner and the bottom of the skillet to disperse the cooking heat. Cook for 50 minutes.

Step 4: Separate the rice from the tahdig and serve

Lift the lid from the pan. There will be condensation trapped under the lid, so avoid tilting it over the rice and inadvertently pouring the steam water back in. Gently scoop the rice onto a serving platter, making sure not to disturb the *tahdig* at the bottom. Loosen the sides of the *tahdig* with a butter knife and flip it onto a plate, or remove from the pan with an offset spatula. Serve whole or broken in pieces.

Rice with Lavash Tahdig

Makes 5¹/₂ cups rice plus one 10-inch disk of tahdig

Lavash is a flatbread eaten in the Middle East and Central Asia. It's the bread that most often accompanies *Sabzi Khordan* (Fresh Herb Platter, page 27), and it's served with kebabs because it's a perfect tool for pulling the meat from the skewer without getting your hands dirty. Lavash comes in large sheets, and it's easy to tear off a piece big enough to fit the bottom of your *tahdig* skillet. It is widely available in Middle Eastern and natural foods markets, but if you can't find it, use pita bread as a substitute.

2 cups white basmati rice
Lavash bread
3 tablespoons refined coconut oil, ghee, or grapeseed oil
2 tablespoons water
¹/₂ teaspoon sea salt

Step 1: Parcook the rice

Soak the rice in cold water for 30 minutes. Swish the rice around a few times, then drain and rinse the rice in cold water until the rinse water runs clear. In a stockpot, combine 8 cups water and 2 heaping tablespoons salt and bring to a boil. Add the rice and return to a boil, uncovered, as it can easily boil over. After 5 minutes, test a grain of the rice by breaking it in half. The rice is ready when it's soft but the center is still opaque and not fully cooked. Drain and rinse the rice under cold water to stop the cooking. Measure out 2 cups rice and set aside.

Step 2: Line the skillet with the lavash

Heat a deep, 10-inch cast iron skillet or enamel paella pan over low heat for a few minutes. Cut out a piece of lavash to cover the bottom of the skillet. If you want to be exact, trace the skillet on the lavash with a knife before you begin to cook. Add the oil (if your skillet is bigger than 10 inches, add an additional 2 tablespoons oil). Fit the bread into the pan. If the lavash goes up the sides of the skillet a little ways, just oil the sides of the skillet to prevent burning. If you're using pita bread instead of lavash, cut it in pieces so it covers the pan in a single layer. Even if the pita bread is patchworked with odd-size pieces, you'll still get *tahdig* that's even and intact. Drizzle the bread with 1 tablespoon of the water.

Step 3: Make the tahdig layer

Spread the 2 cups reserved rice evenly over the bread, and drizzle with the remaining 1 tablespoon water. Pack it down tightly with an offset spatula or large wooden spoon. Sprinkle the sea salt over the rice.

Step 4: Shape the rice into a pyramid and cook

Add the rest of the rice and shape it into a pyramid. Poke several holes in the rice with a chopstick to let steam escape. Cover and turn the heat up to medium-high. Cook the rice for 10 minutes, then turn down the heat to very low and place a clean dish towel or *damkoni* (see page 133) under the lid to catch condensation, and cover the pan tightly. If you have a flame tamer, put it between the burner and the bottom of the skillet to disperse the cooking heat. Cook for 50 minutes.

Step 5: Separate the rice from the tahdig and serve

Lift the lid from the pan. There will be condensation trapped under the lid, so avoid tilting it over the rice and inadvertently pouring the steam water back in. Gently scoop the rice onto a serving platter, making sure not to disturb the *tahdig* at the bottom. Loosen the sides of the *tahdig* with a butter knife and flip it onto a plate, or remove from the pan with an offset spatula. Serve whole or broken in pieces.

Rice with Potato Tahdig

Makes 5 1/2 cups rice plus one 10-inch disk of tahdig

Potato *tahdig* is a rare treat. The potatoes get sweeter and their flavor intensifies as they caramelize. After you line the bottom of the skillet with the potatoes, you may have some leftover slices, but don't try to crowd them in. It's important the potatoes are in a single layer, otherwise your *tahdig* won't cook evenly. Use the extra potatoes for a different recipe, or panfry them on their own and use them to garnish the rice.

3 tablespoons refined coconut oil, ghee, or grapeseed oil
1 large Yukon gold potato or
2 medium red potatoes, peeled and sliced into 1/4-inch-thick rounds
2 cups white basmati rice
Sea salt

Step 1: Parcook the rice

Soak the rice in cold water for 30 minutes. Swish the rice around a few times, then drain and rinse the rice in cold water until it runs clear. In a stockpot, combine 8 cups water and 2 heaping tablespoons salt and bring to a boil. Add the rice and return to a boil, uncovered, as it can easily boil over. After 5 minutes, test a grain of the rice by breaking it in half. The rice is ready when it's soft but the center is still opaque and not fully cooked. Drain and rinse the rice under cold water to stop the cooking. Measure out 2 cups rice and set aside.

Step 2: Line the skillet with the potatoes

Heat a deep, 10-inch cast-iron skillet or enamel paella pan over low heat for a few minutes. Add the oil (if your skillet is bigger than 10 inches, add an additional 2 tablespoons oil). Line the skillet with the potato slices. Fit in as many as you can in a single layer, but make sure that they are all lying flat. Cook uncovered over medium-high heat for 5 minutes. The potatoes should be golden on the first side. Flip the potatoes and season with a pinch of sea salt.

Step 3: Make the tahdig layer

Spread the 2 cups reserved rice evenly over the potatoes, and pack it down tightly with an offset spatula or large wooden spoon. Sprinkle 1/4 teaspoon sea salt over the rice.

Step 4: Shape the rice into a pyramid and cook

Add the rest of the rice and shape it into a pyramid. Poke several holes in the rice with a chopstick to let steam escape. Cover and turn the heat up to medium-high. Cook the rice for 10 minutes, then turn down the heat to very low and place a clean dish towel or *damkoni* (see opposite) under the lid to catch condensation, and cover the pan tightly. If you have a flame tamer, put it between the burner and the bottom of the skillet to disperse the cooking heat. Cook for 50 minutes.

Step 5: Separate the rice from the tahdig and serve

Lift the lid from the pan. There will be condensation trapped under the lid, so avoid tilting it over the rice and inadvertently pouring the steam water back in. Gently scoop the rice onto a serving platter, making sure not to disturb the *tahdig* at the bottom. Loosen the sides of the *tahdig* with a butter knife and flip it onto a plate, or remove from the pan with an offset spatula. Serve whole or broken in pieces.

Cheating with Tahdig

If the idea of cooking perfectly fluffy rice while simultaneously making crunchy, golden *tahdig* on the bottom of the very same pot is too intimidating, never fear. You can always cheat and make the *tahdig* after you've cooked the rice. I sometimes cook a pot of Saffron Rice (page 123), and then make a couple of cups of it into *tahdig*. Because one recipe of Saffron Rice makes just over 7 cups of rice, there's plenty to spare for *tahdig*.

"Faux" Tahdig

Makes one 10-inch disk of tahdig

> *3 tablespoons refined coconut oil, ghee, or extra-light olive oil*
> *2 cups cooked basmati rice*
> *Sea salt*

Line a baking sheet with paper towels or clean dish towels. Heat a deep, 10-inch cast-iron skillet or enamel paella pan over medium-high heat. Add the oil, and then add the rice. Spread the rice evenly over the bottom of the pan, and pack it down tightly with an offset spatula or large wooden spoon. Sprinkle a pinch of salt over the rice. Place a clean dish towel or *damkoni* (see opposite) under the lid to catch condensation, and cover the pan tightly. Cook over medium-high heat for 10 minutes. Turn down the heat to its lowest setting and cook for another 10 minutes.

Lift the lid from the skillet. There may be condensation trapped under the lid, so avoid tilting it over the rice and inadvertently pouring the steam water back in. Loosen the *tahdig* with an offset spatula or a butter knife, and flip it onto the towel-lined baking sheet. Let it rest for a minute or two so the towels absorb the extra cooking oil. Flip it onto a plate and season with a little salt. Serve whole or broken into pieces.

Tahdig Tips and Tricks

Making perfect *tahdig* requires practice and patience, and most people end up with *tahdig* that is either burnt or floppy on the first few tries. Following the pointers below will go a long way toward helping you achieve perfectly crisp and golden *tahdig*.

Preheat the skillet and cooking oil. Preheating the skillet means that when the rice, lavash, or potatoes hit the pan, they immediately start to form a crust, instead of just soaking up the oil. Heat the skillet over low heat for 3 minutes, and then add the oil, followed by the rice. That way, the oil is hot but not smoking.

Start high, go low. Cook the *tahdig* over medium-high heat in the first stage of cooking. If the heat is too low, the *tahdig* won't become crisp. High heat also helps the *tahdig* to absorb the oil. After cooking the *tahdig* over medium-high heat for the first 8 minutes, turn the heat down to very low. Use a flame tamer to make it even lower. This stage serves to dry out the rice, as the steaming process draws the moisture out and into the fabric around the pot lid.

Sneak a peek. Toward the end of cooking, check to see if the *tahdig* is ready by pulling up the rice with an offset spatula or butter knife and peeking underneath. If it looks pale, keep cooking. If it looks dark, you can break off a small piece and check the texture and taste before taking it out of the pan.

Keep it hot. Keep the *tahdig* on low heat until you're ready to serve. If it sits in the pan and cools off it will lose its crisp texture and become rubbery. Ideally, you want to serve it as soon as it's ready.

Special Equipment for Making Tahdig

Damkoni, or towel. A *damkoni* is a padded cloth that fits over the lid of the rice pot to catch condensation as the rice steams. This quirky Persian invention helps the rice to dry out and to become fluffy and separated, as opposed to mushy and wet. A *damkoni* looks like a shower cap, and the ones made in Iran come in the most unlikely bright colors and patterns. But it makes a big difference in getting a good result with *tahdig*.

As a substitute for a *damkoni*, fold up a couple of clean dish towels or paper towels and fit them under the lid, or tie an apron around the lid and fasten it tightly at the top with the strings. When using kitchen towels, make sure they are well out of the way of the burner to avoid a fire.

Flame Tamer. A flame tamer disperses the heat from the burner, making it much less likely that your *tahdig* will burn or cook unevenly. Once you turn down the heat and fit the *damkoni* or towel under the skillet lid, slide the flame tamer between the flame and the bottom of the skillet. The old-fashioned tin flame tamers, or simmer rings, are well made and inexpensive.

Deep Cast-Iron Skillet, or Enameled Paella Pan. Although most people cook *tahdig* using a nonstick pot or pan, I use a deep cast-iron skillet or an enameled paella pan. In fact, cast iron is *more* nonstick than Teflon. I'll be honest: I'm adamant about avoiding nonstick cooking surfaces, which are made with dangerous chemicals proven to be toxic. I heartily encourage you to ditch your nonstick pans—whether they're peeling or not—and embrace cast iron.

Offset Metal Spatula. This is especially handy for packing down the rice to make your *tahdig* layer tight and compact. It also makes it easy to lift up the *tahdig* without breaking it to check if it's done and to remove it from the pan.

rice with sour cherries and almonds

albalu polo

In late June, sour cherries make a brief appearance at American farmers' markets. In Iran, too, come June tangy albalu are enjoyed raw, cooked, and preserved, although they're just as likely to be cooked with meat and grains as they are with sweets. If you don't have fresh sour cherries, look for bottled ones in Polish, Russian, or other eastern European food shops. Bottled sour cherries are preserved in sugar syrup, so taste them for sweetness and adjust the recipe accordingly.

serves 6 to 8

2 cups white basmati rice, soaked in cold water for 1 hour

3 cups water

Sea salt

2 tablespoons butter or unrefined coconut oil, at room temperature

1 pound fresh sour cherries, pitted

1/3 cup honey

1 teaspoon ground cinnamon

1 teaspoon ground cardamom

1 cup slivered or coarsely chopped almonds, toasted

1/2 teaspoon saffron, ground and steeped in 1 tablespoon hot water (see page 15)

Drain the rice and rinse it under cold water until the water runs clear. (Try making *tahdig*! Bring a large pot three-quarters full of salted water to a boil, and follow the instructions on page 128 for making one of four styles of *tahdig*. You'll rejoin this recipe in the next to last paragraph, and mix the sour cherries and almonds with the rice just as if you've been following this recipe all along. Good luck!)

In a stockpot, bring the water to a boil with a pinch of salt. Add the rice, return to a boil, then turn down the heat to its lowest setting. Cover and cook for 20 minutes. Turn off the heat and let the rice rest for 5 minutes, then dot with the butter and fluff with a fork. The rice should be dry and fluffy.

While the rice cooks, put the cherries in a skillet and bring to a boil over high heat. Turn down the heat to low, add the honey, cinnamon, cardamom, and 1 teaspoon salt, and simmer for 15 minutes, until the cooking liquid is very thick.

Scoop the rice into a large bowl. Fold in the cherries and their cooking liquid, the almonds, and the saffron. Season with salt and serve warm.

rice with favas and dill

baghali polo

This herb-flecked rice is perfect for spring, when dill and fava beans are in season. Use fresh favas, or substitute frozen lima beans, which are always available. This recipe calls for copious amounts of dill, and cleaning that amount of fresh herbs can be intimidating. I learned to make this dish by watching my cousin Mahin, however, and I was overjoyed when I saw that she did not pull the fronds from the dill stems, but merely chopped the stems finely and threw them into the rice. The flavor of this rice is especially well suited to making Rice with Potato Tahdig (page 131).

serves 4 to 6

3 cups water
Sea salt
2 cups white basmati rice, soaked
   in cold water for 1 hour
2 tablespoons butter or
   unrefined coconut oil,
   at room temperature

1 pound fresh fava beans, shelled
   and peeled, or 1 pound
   frozen lima beans, thawed
2 tablespoons ghee or
   grapeseed oil

2 cups tightly packed minced
   fresh dill
$1/2$ teaspoon saffron, ground and
   steeped in 1 tablespoon hot
   water (see page 15)

Drain the rice and rinse under cold water until the rinse water runs clear. (Try making *tahdig*! Bring a large pot three-quarters full of salted water to a boil and follow the instructions starting on page 128 for making one of four styles of *tahdig*. You'll rejoin this recipe in the next to last paragraph, and mix the favas and dill with the rice just as if you've been following this recipe all along. Good luck!)

In a stockpot, bring the water to a boil with a pinch of salt. Add the rice, return to a boil, then turn down the heat to its lowest setting. Cover and cook for 20 minutes. Turn off the heat and let the rice rest for 5 minutes, then dot with the butter and fluff with a fork. The rice should be dry and fluffy.

While the rice cooks, prepare the favas. Bring a pot of salted water to a boil and prepare a bowl of ice water. Drop the favas into the boiling water, return to a boil, and cook for 2 minutes, or until just tender. Drain, and shock in the ice water.

continued

Heat the ghee in a skillet over medium heat and sauté the favas for 3 minutes, until heated through. Add the dill and cook for about 1 minute, until just wilted. Combine the favas and rice in a large bowl and drizzle in the saffron. Mix gently, season with salt, and serve.

tomato rice with dried limes

estamboli polo

This is Silk Road comfort food at its best. A warming, aromatic rice that's popular with both Indians and Persians, this dish has a soft texture that's closer to risotto than to the usual fluffy pilaf style of Persian rice. This red, ginger-scented rice borrows from both Indian and Persian pantries and is made with ginger and fragrant star anise. Make this on a Sunday and pair it with salad for quick, healthy dinners during the week.

serves 6

$1/4$ cup peanut oil, refined sesame oil, or grapeseed oil

1 large yellow onion, finely diced

3 cloves garlic, minced

2-inch piece fresh ginger, peeled and minced

1 teaspoon ground turmeric

1 whole star anise

2 cups canned crushed tomatoes (one 16-ounce can) or finely diced fresh tomatoes

2 teaspoons sea salt

3 dried limes, soaked in $1/2$ cup hot water for 15 minutes

3 cups chicken stock or water, boiling

2 cups brown basmati rice, soaked in cold water for 1 hour

Preheat the oven to 375°F.

Heat the oil over medium heat in a Dutch oven or a large, ovenproof skillet, add the onion, and sauté for about 15 minutes, until lightly browned. Add the garlic, ginger, turmeric, star anise, tomatoes, and salt to the onion. Pierce the limes and add them and their soaking water to the Dutch oven, followed by the stock. Simmer, uncovered, for 5 minutes. Press the limes against the side of the pan with a spoon to help release their flavor.

Drain the rice and rinse under cold water until the water runs clear. Add the rice to the Dutch oven, bring the mixture to a boil, then turn off the heat. Cover and place it on a baking sheet before carefully transferring to the oven. Bake for $1^1/2$ hours. When the rice is done, let it rest at room temperature, covered, for 20 minutes. Fluff with a fork, remove the limes and anise, season with salt, and serve.

persian shepherd's pie

tah chin

I call this dish Persian Shepherd's Pie because, like the British favorite, it's a one-pot meal that's served up in hearty slices. The idea here is to combine cooked rice with meat and vegetables and bake the mixture like a casserole. When done, the rice should be firm on top, with a crust of golden tahdig on the bottom. I use a 12-inch cast-iron skillet because it yields more luscious tahdig than a smaller pan. When marinated overnight, the meat has a chance to soak up the flavor of the saffron, so start this dish the day before. Serve with Mixed Vegetable Pickle (page 178) and Yogurt with Shallots (page 36).

serves 8

6 tablespoons grapeseed oil
1 yellow onion, diced
8 ounces Yukon gold potatoes, peeled and finely diced
1 teaspoon ground turmeric
Sea salt and freshly ground black pepper

1 pound skinless chicken or turkey thighs, or halved breasts, bone-in
2¹/₂ cups thick Greek-style yogurt
1 teaspoon saffron, ground and steeped in 1 tablespoon hot water (see page 15)

Grated zest and juice of 1 lemon
2 eggs
3 cups white basmati rice
¹/₄ cup barberries, soaked in water for ¹/₂ hour and drained, or dried sour cherries

Preheat the oven to 450°F. Use grapeseed oil to grease a baking sheet.

In a large bowl, combine the onion and potatoes. Season with the turmeric, 1 teaspoon salt, and 1 teaspoon pepper, and spread in the center of the baking sheet. Season the chicken generously with salt and pepper, and place it on top of the vegetables. Cover with foil and roast for 20 minutes. Uncover and roast for 10 minutes, or until the vegetables are tender and the chicken is cooked through. Let cool, then bone the chicken and cut the meat into 1-inch pieces.

In a large bowl, whisk together the yogurt, saffron, lemon juice, and zest. Add 1 teaspoon salt and 1 teaspoon pepper. Whisk in the eggs, then transfer ¹/₂ cup of the marinade to a sealed container and refrigerate. Add the chicken and vegetables to the remainder and stir to coat with the marinade. Cover and refrigerate overnight.

continued

Soak the rice in cold water for 30 minutes, then drain and rinse in cold water until the water runs clear.

In a stockpot, combine the water and 2 heaping tablespoons salt and bring to a boil. Add the rice and return to a boil, uncovered. After 3 minutes, test a grain of rice by breaking it in half. The rice is ready when it's soft but the center is still opaque and not fully cooked. Drain and rinse the rice under cold water to stop the cooking.

In a large bowl, combine the reserved 1/2 cup marinade with half of the rice. Heat a 10- to 12-inch Dutch oven or cast-iron skillet over medium heat. Add 4 tablespoons of the oil. Spread the rice mixture over the bottom and 1 to 2 inches up the sides. With a slotted spoon, lift the chicken and vegetables from the marinade and spread them evenly over the rice. Spoon 1/4 cup of the marinade over the chicken and vegetables, and sprinkle with the barberries. Season with salt and pepper. Spread the rest of the rice over the chicken and vegetables, and spoon the remaining marinade over the top. Smooth the rice with a spatula, gently working in the marinade. Drizzle with the remaining 2 tablespoons oil.

Cover the pan tightly and cook over medium heat for 8 minutes, then turn down the heat to very low. If you have a flame tamer, put it between the burner and the skillet to disperse the cooking heat. Cook for 1 1/4 hours. Turn off the heat and let the pie rest, covered, for 15 minutes.

Loosen the sides of the pie with a butter knife and slice into wedges. Or, for a more dramatic presentation, flip the pie onto a baking sheet, then transfer to a platter to serve.

Vegetarian Option

Substitute diced mushrooms for the chicken, and follow the same instructions for the cooking the chicken with the vegetables. After roasting, drain off the cooking liquid before adding the vegetables to the marinade.

quinoa with french lentils, wild rice, and golden raisins

Nutty quinoa and wild rice are New World ingredients, but they easily fit the Persian formula for livening up a grain with contrasting textures and flavors. Because of the addition of plump, peppery French lentils, this dish is hearty enough to serve as a meal. Cook the wild rice separately, as it takes about an hour to cook through fully, almost twice the time needed for the rest of the ingredients. You can cook the wild rice and the onions the day before. If you have leftovers, make them into a satisfying salad by adding balsamic vinegar, fresh herbs, and lettuce.

serves 6

1/2 cup wild rice, rinsed
1/4 cup French lentils, picked over
    and rinsed
Sea salt
3 cups vegetable stock, chicken
    stock, or water

1 cup quinoa, rinsed
1 yellow onion, diced
3 tablespoons ghee or
    grapeseed oil
2 cups golden raisins

2 tablespoons butter, at room
    temperature
1/2 teaspoon saffron, ground and
    steeped in 1 tablespoon hot
    water (see page 15)
Freshly ground black pepper

Fill a saucepan halfway with water and bring to a boil. Add the wild rice, lentils, and a pinch of salt. Lower the heat and simmer, covered, for 1 hour. Drain and reserve.

Return the saucepan to the stove, add the stock, and bring to a boil. Add the quinoa and 1 teaspoon salt and return to a boil. Lower the heat and simmer, covered, for 30 minutes, until the quinoa is tender. Let rest off the heat for 10 minutes, then fluff with a fork.

While the quinoa cooks, heat a skillet over medium heat and add the ghee. Add the onion and sauté for 15 minutes, until it is lightly browned. Add the raisins and cook for 3 to 5 minutes, until heated through.

In a large bowl, combine the onion and raisins with the wild rice and quinoa. Add the butter and saffron and toss gently. Season to taste with salt and pepper and serve at room temperature.

sweets

The range and quality of Persian desserts is stunning, from the melt-in-your-mouth majesty of saffron rice pudding to the icy pink goodness of *faloodeh*. The dessert recipes in this chapter emphasize the luscious fruits and nuts of the Iranian Plateau, but they also embrace a wide variety of culinary influences from all along the Silk Road.

If there's one dish that personifies this double life of Persian desserts, it's surely the cookie known as *kiloocheh*, a date-and-walnut-filled delicacy that easily can be thought of as a Middle Eastern Fig Newton. *Koloocheh* are round baked Persian pastries that are usually stamped with a wheel pattern and filled with a spiced mixture of dried fruit and nuts. The result is a rich crust and a sweet, jammy interior.

Variations of *koloocheh* appear in many of the cultures along the Silk Road. Buddhists, Christians, and Muslims, as well as Jews, all have their unique take on its basic design. In China, for example, the midautumn harvest festival is celebrated with the iconic moon cake, an intricately molded pastry shell stuffed with a sweet or savory filling. Just as closely related are the eastern European cookies called *kolachy* or *kalacs*, which are filled with jam, poppy seeds, or walnuts. In the Arabic world, *ma'amoul* cookies are ornately shaped in intricate wooden molds and stuffed with dates and walnuts. They, too, are popular holiday treats for Muslims, Christians, and Jews throughout the Middle East. Their honey-soaked cousins, *makroud*, in Tunisia are an essential part of the North African celebrations that mark the end of Ramadan.

My version of *koloocheh* on page 155 attempts to streamline the often laborious process involved in making them, requiring no tricky pastry mold or arcane filling techniques. I've also included fresh variations of other traditional Persian desserts, such as Chickpea and Almond Flour Icebox Cookies (opposite), Amaranth Rice Pudding with Rose Water (page 157), and Rhubarb and Rose Water Sorbet with Rice Noodles (page 147). Some of these recipes pair beloved Persian ingredients with more European-style desserts, like No-Bake Persimmon and Goat Cheese Cheesecake (page 159), Pomegranate Semifreddo with Blood Orange Compote (page 148), and Nutty Chocolate Bark with Cardamom and Coffee (page 161). Several of these sweet treats are gluten-free and can be made with natural sweeteners.

chickpea and almond flour icebox cookies

nan-e nokhodchi

Traditionally, these cookies are made exclusively with chickpea flour and punched out with tiny shamrock-shaped cookie cutters, but the dough is soft and warms up quickly, so I like to shape it into a bar, chill until firm, and then slice it into cookies. I add almond flour because it makes the dough sturdier and mellows the distinct bean taste of the chickpea flour. The bar of dough can be made ahead and chilled in the refrigerator for up to 3 days.

makes about 40 cookies

¹/₂ cup unsalted butter, at room temperature
¹/₂ cup organic cane sugar
1 teaspoon rose water

¹/₂ cup plus 3 tablespoons chickpea flour
¹/₂ cup plus 3 tablespoons almond flour

1 teaspoon ground cardamom
¹/₂ teaspoon ground cinnamon
¹/₄ teaspoon sea salt
3 tablespoons pistachios, coarsely ground

Cream together the butter and sugar with an electric mixer. Beat in the rose water for a few seconds. Whisk together the flours, cardamom, cinnamon, and salt in a separate bowl, and beat into the butter in two batches, until just combined. Turn the dough out onto a piece of plastic wrap and press it into a disk. Wrap and chill in the freezer for 30 minutes.

Remove the dough from the freezer, unwrap it, and lay it in the middle of a large piece of plastic wrap or wax paper. Fold the wrap or paper over the dough. Form the dough into a log approximately 10 inches in length and 1¹/₂ inches in diameter, then square off the long sides to form a bar. Chill in the refrigerator until the dough is very firm, at least 2 hours.

Preheat the oven to 350°F. Line two baking sheets with parchment paper.

Slice the bar into cookies ¹/₄ inch thick and place them on the prepared baking sheets, spacing them 1 inch apart. Press a pinch of pistachios into the center of each cookie.

Bake the cookies until the bottoms are just golden, 15 to 18 minutes. Let cool on the pans for 5 minutes, then transfer to cooling racks. The cookies can be stored in a sealed container at room temperature for up to 5 days.

rhubarb and rose water sorbet with rice noodles

faloodeh

On the streets of Tehran you'll find food vendors selling dishes of chewy frozen vermicelli suspended in an icy white sherbet with a perfumed scent. This whimsical treat is called faloodeh, and is one of the earliest known frozen desserts, dating as far back as 400 BCE. Faloodeh is typically white, but this version is colored bright pink by a compote of rhubarb. A drizzle of something tart, like sour cherry syrup or lime juice, brings this dessert vividly to life.

serves 6 to 8

2 ounces rice vermicelli
1 pound rhubarb stalks, preferably red, coarsely chopped
¹/₄ cup water
1¹/₂ cups organic cane sugar

1 teaspoon sea salt
1 tablespoon rose water
3 tablespoons freshly squeezed lime juice, plus extra for garnish

Crushed pistachios, for garnish
Sour cherry syrup (page 169), for garnish (optional)

Put the vermicelli in a bowl. Bring a pot of lightly salted water to a boil, and pour over the vermicelli. Soak for 4 minutes, until tender. Drain and rinse under cold water. Cut the vermicelli into 1-inch lengths.

In a saucepan, combine the rhubarb with the water, sugar, and salt. Bring to a boil, stirring to dissolve the sugar. Cover and lower the heat to a simmer. Cook for about 10 minutes, until the rhubarb is very soft. Let cool completely.

Pour the rhubarb into a blender. Add the rose water and lime juice and blend until smooth. Stir the vermicelli and rhubarb together in a large bowl. Pour into a shallow baking dish and freeze, uncovered.

Rake the *faloodeh* with a fork after 2 hours to prevent it from freezing into a solid mass. Freeze and stir again after 2 hours. Repeat after another 2 hours, if necessary. The *faloodeh* will have a malleable consistency, somewhere between ice cream and sorbet, within 4 to 6 hours. Scoop it into serving bowls and top with pistachios and lime juice. Drizzle with sour cherry syrup, if desired. The *faloodeh* tastes best within 24 hours of being made.

pomegranate semifreddo with blood orange compote

This frozen pink mousse has a frilly green petticoat of pistachios and a scarlet-orange cloak of blood oranges and pomegranate seeds. It looks quite delicate but is simple to make. Be sure to assemble the semifreddo the day before serving it, because it takes several hours to freeze. When serving, have a pot of very hot water and a clean kitchen towel ready. You'll need them to warm your knife and wipe it dry to cut through the semifreddo easily.

serves 8 to 10

SEMIFREDDO
1/2 cup pistachios, toasted and
    coarsely chopped
1 3/4 cups heavy whipping cream
1 cup organic cane sugar

7 large egg yolks
1 teaspoon ground cardamom
1/4 teaspoon sea salt
2 teaspoons rose water
1/2 cup pomegranate molasses

COMPOTE
Seeds of 1 pomegranate
    (see page 62)
3 blood oranges, peeled and
    diced
1 to 2 tablespoons honey

To make the semifreddo, line a 9 by 5 by 3-inch loaf pan with parchment paper, so that the parchment hangs over each side of the pan. You'll need to cut one long, narrow piece to cover the bottom, and one long, wide piece to cover the sides. Spread the pistachios over the bottom of the pan.

In an electric mixer fitted with the whisk attachment, whip the cream on medium speed until it forms soft peaks. Transfer to a different bowl, and store in the refrigerator. Replace the bowl on the mixer without washing.

Whisk the sugar, egg yolks, cardamom, and salt in a large stainless-steel bowl. Set the bowl over a large saucepan of gently boiling water and whisk for about 6 minutes, until the sugar is melted, the yolks are thick, and an instant-read thermometer inserted into the mixture reads 170°F.

Transfer the yolk mixture to the mixer bowl. Using the whisk attachment, beat on medium speed for 5 to 6 minutes, until cool and thick. Drizzle the rose water on top and fold in the whipped cream. Swirl in the pomegranate molasses.

Transfer the mixture to the prepared pan, and tap the pan on a hard surface to remove any air pockets. Cover with a piece of parchment paper. Freeze for 8 to 12 hours, until firm.

To make the compote, combine the pomegranate seeds, blood oranges, and honey and chill in the refrigerator for 1 to 2 hours.

To serve, remove the parchment from the top of the *semifreddo*. Dip a small knife into hot water, wipe it dry, and run the knife along the inside edge of the pan to loosen the *semifreddo*, then invert the pan onto a cutting board and lift off the pan. Now dip a large knife into the hot water, wipe it dry, and cut the *semifreddo* into 1-inch-thick slices, rewarming the knife as needed. Accompany each serving with a few spoonfuls of compote.

saffron frozen yogurt and cardamom pizzelle sandwiches

bastani

This tart, citrusy frozen yogurt is luscious on its own, or in a Persian-style ice cream sandwich between a couple of cardamom pizzelles. These pizzelles are slightly flexible, in order to accommodate the frozen yogurt without breaking. For crispier pizzelles, let them cook for a minute or more, until they're golden. I prefer these sandwiches to be petite, so I make the pizzelles with a 3-inch-wide pizzelle mold. (For information on where to find my pizzelle maker, see Resources, page 189).

makes 4 cups frozen yogurt and about 12 three-inch pizzelles
(enough for about 6 sandwiches plus an extra 1 cup yogurt)

FROZEN YOGURT
1 1/2 cups organic cane sugar
1/4 teaspoon saffron
Grated zest of 2 large oranges
4 cups thick Greek-style yogurt
1/4 teaspoon sea salt

PIZZELLES
1 egg
2 tablespoons organic cane sugar
Pinch of sea salt
2 tablespoons refined coconut
  oil, melted

1 to 2 teaspoons orange flower
  water (optional)
1/2 cup spelt flour
1/2 teaspoon baking powder
1 teaspoon ground cardamom

To make the frozen yogurt, grind the sugar and saffron to a fine powder in an electric spice grinder, and transfer to a large bowl. Add the orange zest, yogurt, and salt, and stir well. Freeze in an ice cream maker according to the manufacturer's instructions.

To make the pizzelle batter, whisk the egg in a bowl with the sugar, salt, oil, and orange flower water. In a separate bowl, mix together the flour, baking powder, and cardamom. Whisk the dry ingredients into the wet ingredients until smooth.

Heat a pizzelle iron according to the manufacturer's instructions and grease it very lightly with coconut oil. Drop the batter onto the hot iron by the tablespoonful. Close the iron and cook for 30 to 60 seconds, depending on your machine. Loosen the pizzelles with a knife and let cool on a flat surface. Repeat with the remaining batter, greasing the iron as needed. The pizzelles will last for a few days in an airtight container at room temperature.

continued

To make the sandwiches, place a scoop of frozen yogurt between two pizzelles. Allow the sandwiches to firm up in the freezer for at least 15 minutes, or up to 24 hours, before serving. The yogurt gets very hard after a day in the freezer, but it softens up after about 10 minutes at room temperature. The extra frozen yogurt can be eaten on its own or topped with fresh fruit, and it makes a creamy and flavorful base for smoothies.

The Festive Table: The Tradition of the Sofreh

Imagine a large table covered by a fine cloth, decorated with sweets, bread, flowers, candles, fruit, a book of poetry, and a mirror. No, it's not the snack table in the waiting room of an expensive spa. This is a *sofreh*, a "spread" in Persian, and it refers to the ancient Zoroastrian custom of spreading a cloth on the ground during special occasions and covering it with symbolic elements. Up until recently, it was customary for Iranians to take their meals seated on the floor, where a *sofreh* cloth would be laid out on a rug and spread with food. This is the origin of the *sofreh*, and though many people still eat in this fashion, the highly ornate *sofreh* tables that appear at holidays and at weddings are strictly intended for ritual purposes.

Along with many other Zoroastrian customs, the use of the *sofreh* was enfolded into Shia Muslim practice after Iran became an Islamic country, and it's typical for the ritual table to hold a copy of the Koran. The *sofreh* is meant to embody the prayers and hopes of a family, couple, or individual.

The objects placed on the *sofreh* change according to the occasion, with the most elaborate and expensive designs typically trotted out for weddings. (Having helped create a *sofreh* for my own wedding, I'm intimately familiar with the details!)

Some of the symbolic items that are featured on the wedding *sofreh*, known as the *sofreh-ye aghd*, include the following:

- A mirror, symbolizing reality and honesty
- Persian cookies and candy, to symbolize the sweetness of life
- Honey, also for sweetness; after signing the marriage documents, the bride and groom feed each other honey with their fingers

The *sofreh* also plays a key role during the Iranian New Year celebration, known as *Norooz* (for a full explanation of *Norooz*, see page 91). Walk into any Persian home between mid-March and the first week of April and you'll find a table decorated with pots of wheatgrass sprouts, a goldfish in a bowl (it can be real or fake), a book of Hafez's poetry, and seven foods that begin with the letter *s* in Persian, each of which has a distinct role in encouraging the divine spirit to bring good things in the year ahead.

Some of the symbolic items that belong on the *sofreh-ye haft-seen*, the "*sofreh* of the seven s's," include the following:

- Garlic (*seer*), symbolizing medicine
- Green herbs (*sabzeh*) for rebirth
- Sumac (*somagh*), reflecting the color of the sunrise, and the victory of light and goodness over the dark
- Vinegar (*serkeh*) for patience and longevity

mulberry yogurt cake

Growing up in Philadelphia, we had a mulberry tree in our backyard, and my father was always content when he could come home on a June evening and eat fresh berries right off the tree, just like he did in Iran. I assumed that everyone ate mulberries until I came to New York and saw that only the birds seemed to like them! Sweet mulberries are in season in May and June, but if you can't find them use blackberries (large blackberries should be halved before baking). Whipping the egg whites gives lightness to this fruity cake, and low-gluten barley flour gives it a tender texture.

makes one 10-inch cake

2 cups barley flour
2 teaspoons baking soda
$^1/_2$ teaspoon cinnamon
$^1/_2$ teaspoon sea salt
$^1/_2$ cup unrefined coconut oil, melted and cooled to room temperature

$^1/_2$ cup thick Greek-style yogurt
2 eggs, separated
Zest of 1 lemon
$^1/_2$ teaspoon vanilla extract

$1^1/_4$ cups organic cane sugar
$^1/_2$ teaspoon freshly squeezed lemon juice
2 cups mulberries

Preheat the oven to 350°F. Grease a 10-inch springform pan.

In a medium bowl, whisk together the flour, baking soda, cinnamon, and $^1/_4$ teaspoon salt. In a large bowl, whisk together the coconut oil, yogurt, egg yolks, lemon zest, vanilla, and 1 cup of the sugar. Stir the dry ingredients into the wet until just combined.

In an electric mixture fitted with the whisk attachment, beat the egg whites with the remaining $^1/_4$ teaspoon salt on medium-high speed. After about 3 minutes, when they start to foam and puff, add the lemon juice and continue beating until they form soft peaks. Add the remaining $^1/_4$ cup sugar and beat for 3 to 4 minutes, until the whites are stiff and shiny.

Fold one-third of the egg whites into the batter to loosen it slightly, then fold in the rest. Gently fold in the berries. Pour the batter into the springform pan and bake for 1 hour and 10 minutes, or until a toothpick inserted into the center comes out clean. Let cool completely in the pan on a cooling rack. Store at room temperature for up to 3 days.

date-and-walnut-filled cookies

koloocheh

These butter cookies are unmistakably Middle Eastern: Persian Jews make them at Purim, while Arabic Christians eat a similar cookie at Easter, as do Muslims during various Eid celebrations. The key to getting the cookies to keep their shape is to refrigerate them until firm after filling and shaping. The combination of gluten-free flours here produces a nutty taste and a light texture, but you can use an equivalent amount of white flour.

makes about 18 cookies

DOUGH
1 cup unsalted butter or
    refined coconut oil, at room
    temperature
$1/3$ cup plus $1/2$ cup organic cane
    sugar
1 teaspoon vanilla extract
1 egg

$3/4$ cup fava bean flour
$3/4$ cup coconut flour
$1/2$ cup tapioca flour
$1/2$ teaspoon sea salt
1 teaspoon ground cardamom
2 teaspoons baking powder

FILLING
$1/2$ cup finely chopped walnuts
$1/2$ cup Medjool dates, pitted and
    chopped
$1/2$ teaspoon ground cinnamon
$1/4$ cup freshly squeezed orange
    juice
2 tablespoons honey
Pinch of sea salt

To make the dough, in an electric mixer fitted with the paddle attachment, cream together the butter and sugar on medium-high speed for about 3 minutes, until light and fluffy. Add the vanilla and egg and mix until just combined. In a separate bowl, whisk together the flours, salt, cardamom, and baking powder. Add the dry ingredients to the wet ingredients in two batches, stopping to scrape down the sides of the bowl as needed. Turn the dough onto a piece of plastic wrap and press it into a disk. Wrap and chill in the refrigerator for 2 hours, until firm but still flexible.

To make the filling, combine $1/4$ cup of the walnuts with the dates, cinnamon, orange juice, honey, and salt in a small saucepan and bring to a boil. Lower the heat and simmer uncovered, stirring often, for 5 to 7 minutes, until the mixture forms a thick paste. Transfer to a plate and let cool to room temperature.

Line two baking sheets with parchment paper.

continued

To make each cookie, wet your hands and break off a lemon-size piece of the dough. Flatten the dough, or make a well in it using your thumb. Place $1/2$ teaspoon of the filling in the middle, then pinch the dough closed and roll it into a ball. Flatten the dough gently between your palms to form a disk 1 inch thick, and place it on the lined baking sheet. Press a pinch of the remaining $1/4$ cup walnuts into the center of the cookie. Repeat with the remaining dough and filling.

Refrigerate the cookies for 45 minutes, until firm. While the cookies chill, preheat the oven to 350°F.

Bake the cookies for 25 minutes, until the undersides are golden. Transfer to a cooling rack and let cool completely. In a clean spice grinder, grind the remaining $1/2$ cup sugar into a fine powder. Dust the cookies with the powdered sugar and serve. Store in an airtight container at room temperature for up to 5 days.

amaranth rice pudding with rose water

sholeh zard

This sweet grain pudding is delicately spiced with a combination of saffron, cinnamon, and rose water. Chewy, nutty amaranth grains combined with the rice give it a surprising texture. Although basmati rice is usually soaked before cooking to get rid of the extra starch, there's no need to soak it here because the starch helps to bind the pudding. Sholeh zard is usually served cold, so make it ahead of time, even the day before, to give it ample time to cool. Persian cooks use ground cinnamon to decorate the pudding's surface with patterns, paisleys, and auspicious sayings, so get creative with stencils and designs and have fun with it.

serves 6

$^1/_3$ cup amaranth
$^1/_3$ cup white or brown basmati
    rice
6 cups water
$^1/_4$ teaspoon sea salt
1 cup organic cane sugar

1 teaspoon ground cardamom
3 tablespoons unsalted butter
$^1/_2$ teaspoon saffron, ground and
    steeped in 1 tablespoon hot
    water (see page 15)

1 tablespoon rose water
Ground cinnamon, for garnish
Crushed pistachios, for garnish

In a large, deep skillet, combine the amaranth, rice, water, and salt and bring to a boil; watch carefully because it can boil over easily. Lower the heat and simmer, covered, for 25 minutes, until the grains are very soft.

Uncover the skillet and add the sugar, cardamom, and butter. Simmer, uncovered, for about 30 minutes, until most of the water is cooked out and the porridge is thick, stirring often. Add the saffron and rose water and cook for 3 more minutes.

Spoon the pudding into individual bowls or one large serving bowl and let cool to room temperature. Cover and store in the refrigerator until ready to serve. Shake cinnamon over the top, garnish with pistachios, and serve.

no-bake persimmon and goat cheese cheesecake

Whenever I bring home persimmons, I always imagine that I'll work them into an artful, sophisticated dish. But their coral color and honeysuckle flavor are so alluring that as soon as they ripen, I invariably tear into one raw, scooping out the flesh in sheer, uninhibited delight. Perhaps that's why I've created a dessert that leaves the pure flavor of persimmons intact. This airy cheesecake requires no cooking, and the sauce is simply pureed persimmons. Make the cheesecake at least 4 hours before serving, or even the day before, so it's firm and easy to slice. Try substituting ripe mangoes or peaches for the persimmons; because both of these fruits hold their shape, you can puree enough to go inside the cake and dice the rest to use as a topping.

makes one 10-inch cake

1/2 cup heavy cream
1 1/2 cups pistachios, toasted
1 cup crushed graham crackers
3/4 cup plus 3 tablespoons unrefined coconut oil, melted and cooled

1/2 teaspoon ground cinnamon
1 1/2 teaspoons ground cardamom
1 cup plus 2 tablespoons organic cane sugar
Sea salt

5 very ripe hachiya persimmons
1 pound fresh goat cheese, at room temperature, crumbled
1 tablespoon freshly squeezed lime juice

Lightly oil a 10-inch springform pan with coconut oil.

In the bowl of an electric mixer fitted with the whisk attachment, whip the cream into stiff peaks. Transfer to a small bowl and set aside in the refrigerator. Replace the mixer bowl without washing.

In a food processor, combine the pistachios and graham crackers with 3 tablespoons of the coconut oil, the cinnamon, the cardamom, and 2 tablespoons of the sugar. Add a pinch of salt and pulse until the mixture clumps easily. Transfer to the springform pan and spread evenly over the bottom. Press down with the bottom of a juice glass to pack it down evenly.

Scoop the flesh from the persimmons and puree in a blender until smooth. Set aside 1/2 cup of the puree, and store the rest in the refrigerator.

continued

Combine the goat cheese, the remaining $^3/_4$ cup coconut oil, and the remaining 1 cup sugar in the mixer fitted with the whisk attachment and beat for 2 to 3 minutes, until smooth. Fold in the $^1/_2$ cup persimmon puree, the lime juice, and a pinch of salt. Fold in the whipped cream. Pour the mixture into the springform pan and smooth the top. Chill in the refrigerator for at least 4 hours, until firm.

To serve, remove the pan sides and cut the cheesecake into wedges. Garnish each serving with a generous spoonful of the persimmon puree. The cheesecake will keep in the refrigerator for up to 4 days.

nutty chocolate bark with cardamom and coffee

This festive chocolate confection is inspired by the combination of cardamom and coffee, as seen in the recipe for Cardamom Coffee (page 169). You can find dried mulberries at natural foods stores and at the Persian food suppliers listed in the Resources section (page 189). (See photo of cardamom pods and dried mulberries on page 118.)

makes about 20 pieces

2 cups semisweet chocolate chips, or 1 (16-ounce) bittersweet chocolate bar, broken into pieces
1 teaspoon ground cardamom
$^1/_4$ cup dried mulberries

$^1/_4$ cup dried tart cherries
$^3/_4$ cup almonds, toasted and coarsely chopped
$^1/_2$ cup pistachios, toasted and coarsely chopped

2 teaspoons coffee beans, coarsely chopped
Pinch of coarse salt, such as fleur de sel, Maldon salt, or kosher salt

Grease a baking sheet and line it with parchment paper.

Melt the chocolate in a large stainless-steel bowl placed over (not touching) simmering water in a pot. Add the cardamom and stir to dissolve for a couple of minutes. Turn off the heat and stir in half of the mulberries, cherries, almonds, and pistachios.

Remove the bowl from the heat and dry the bottom with a towel. Pour the chocolate onto the prepared baking sheet. With an offset spatula or rubber spatula, spread the chocolate in a wide rectangle about $^1/_4$ inch thick. Sprinkle with the remaining nuts, dried fruit, and the coffee beans, and press them gently into the chocolate. Dust with the salt.

Cool in the refrigerator for about 2 hours, until hard. When firm, slide the chocolate onto a cutting board and cut or break it into pieces. The chocolate gets soft quickly in warm weather, so keep it refrigerated until just before serving.

beverages

Today's popular Persian drinks include the minty carbonated yogurt beverage *doogh* (page 165); various fruit-flavored soda pops; and an impressive variety of nonalcoholic beer and malt beverages, such as the ubiquitous Istak. Slightly more traditional, but no less fun, are the fresh cold drinks called *sharbat*, from which we derive the words "sherbet," "sorbet," and "syrup." These lightly sweetened drinks are made from fruit and flower essences, and, like malt beverages, are touted for their various health benefits. The Sour Cherry Spritzer (page 168), Naturally Sweet Dried Lime Tea (page 170), and watermelon-infused *Sekanjabin* (page 173) featured in this book are all examples of refreshing *sharbat*.

Things get a little trickier when talking about grown-up drinks. A strict ban on alcohol has been in place in Iran since the 1979 revolution, and alcohol consumption has been discouraged for centuries, so for many Persians, the pairing of wine and food is relatively uncharted territory. Still, it's worth noting that Persia was one of the earliest wine-making cultures and was renowned for the excellent quality of its date, rose, and grape wines. Shiraz, the home of Iran's famous poet and wine lover Hafez, is still popularly known as "the city of wine and roses," and wine was an integral aspect of religious ritual for the Zoroastrian faithful.

As a general rule, wines from countries geographically close to Iran—Lebanon, Morocco, Portugal, Spain, and even southern Italy—complement Persian food extremely well, as do many California wines. Some people find that a slightly sweet white wine, such as a Riesling, nicely sets off the fruit, flower, and citrus flavors in many dishes, while others prefer a heartier, earthier red to stand up to the full-bodied flavors of Persian meat dishes. And while French Syrah and Australian Shiraz grapes have not been authoritatively linked to the Shiraz region of Iran, the simple linguistic connection makes Shiraz a compelling choice for many.

In theory, a Persian meal should always conclude with glasses of hot *chai*. Not to be confused with Indian *chai*, this is a potent black tea that Persians brew several times a day, especially after big meals, and casually sip with small nuggets of *nabat*, or rock sugar. (If you're sensitive to caffeine, be warned: this supercharged digestif will keep you animated for hours!) In keeping with the Persian tradition of medicinal drinks, I've also included a recipe for a Winter Orchard Tea (page 171) that you can serve on its own or mix with black tea for an extra caffeine boost. And as an homage to Persian ice cream, I offer the *Majoon* shake (Date Shake with Toasted Nuts, page 167), a rich frozen treat made with unexpected Eastern flavors—part cooling beverage and part decadent dessert.

salty mint yogurt soda

doogh

Here in America, salty soda is a contradiction in terms, yet the Japanese love their salty plum soda, Indians hydrate with a salted lime thirst-quencher, and Finns flavor their cocktails with a salty black licorice brew. Doogh, which traditionally goes hand in hand with Persian kebab, is a similarly strange concoction of yogurt, salt, and herbs. I loved doogh as a child, and it was my doorway into an exciting new realm of flavors. Give it a try! For the right savory balance, use dried spearmint instead of fresh—find it at Arabic and Persian markets or online (see Resources, page 189). You can also make your own dried spearmint (see page 12). For kosher cooks, enjoy doogh with the tempeh kebabs on page 96. (See photo on page 94.)

serves 4 to 6

2 cups plain yogurt (not thick)
2 teaspoons dried mint
Pinch of sea salt
1/2 teaspoon freshly ground black
    pepper

4 cups seltzer
Ice cubes (optional)
Fresh mint, for garnish

Put the yogurt in a large bowl. Add the dried mint, rubbing it between your palms to release the flavor. Add the salt and pepper, and whisk in the seltzer until the mixture is frothy. If the dried mint leaves are large, put the *doogh* in a blender and blend for 1 minute to break them down a bit. This will make the drink extra frothy, but it's not necessary. Taste and add more salt if desired.

Fill glasses halfway with ice and pour in the *doogh*. Garnish with fresh mint.

date shake with toasted nuts

majoon

I first tasted a majoon *at the Café Glacé in the Westwood neighborhood of Los Angeles, where these decadent concoctions are whipped up with vanilla ice cream for Westwood's large Persian community. I make* majoon *with yogurt instead, which gives it a hint of lemony sourness and packs enough nutrients for a healthy breakfast. Although it takes more time, I recommend toasting nuts and seeds in the oven on a dry baking sheet, rather than in a pan on the stove top, because they cook more evenly. You can toast a few cups at a time and keep them on hand for various recipes. Toast the delicate coconut flakes, sesame seeds, and pistachios at 300°F for 3 to 4 minutes, then transfer immediately to a plate to prevent burning. Toast the almonds and walnuts at 350°F for about 12 minutes, until fragrant and crisp.*

serves 2 to 4 (makes 3¹/₂ cups)

SHAKE
1 banana, peeled and frozen
8 Medjool dates, pitted
¹/₂ cup plain yogurt (not thick)
¹/₂ teaspoon vanilla extract
Pinch of ground cinnamon
Pinch of sea salt
2 cups ice cubes
³/₄ cup to 1 cup water

TOPPINGS
1 tablespoon toasted
    unsweetened coconut flakes
1 tablespoon toasted almonds,
    coarsely chopped
1 tablespoon toasted walnuts,
    coarsely chopped

1 tablespoon toasted pistachios,
    coarsely chopped
1 tablespoon toasted sesame
    seeds

Cut the banana into 1-inch-thick slices and place them in a blender. Add the dates, yogurt, vanilla, cinnamon, salt, ice cubes, and ³/₄ cup water and blend until smooth. Add an additional ¹/₄ cup water if the shake is too thick. Pour into glasses, top with rows of coconut flakes, almonds, walnuts, pistachios, and sesame seeds, and serve.

sour cherry spritzer

This recipe serves one; simply scale it up depending on how many you want to serve.

serves 1

1 tablespoon sour cherry syrup
   (below)
1 tablespoon freshly squeezed
   lime juice

1 tablespoon water
Ice cubes
1 cup seltzer

Mix the syrup, lime juice, and water in a glass. Add ice, pour in the seltzer, and serve.

Sour Cherry Syrup

makes 1¹/₂ cups (enough for 24 spritzers)

The taste of sour cherries is preserved all year long in this sweet-and-sour syrup, a common ingredient in Iran. Sour cherry syrup is used in *sharbat*, fruit essence drinks like the Sour Cherry Spritzer, and as a sauce for the Rhubarb and Rose Water Sorbet with Rice Noodles (page 147). One of the best things about this recipe is that you don't have to pit the cherries! The cherries are cooked with their pits, giving the syrup a more intense, almondy aroma. The pits are then extracted by gently blending just long enough to separate the flesh from the seeds. You shouldn't blend for more than 30 seconds; after that the pits can start to break up and make the syrup bitter.

1¹/₂ *pounds (4 cups) sour cherries, stemmed*
2 *cups water*
2 *cups organic cane sugar*
¹/₄ *teaspoon sea salt*

Combine the cherries and water in a large skillet and bring to a boil. Lower the heat slightly, add the sugar and salt, and stir to dissolve. Boil gently, uncovered, for 40 minutes, stirring occasionally. The mixture will be slightly thickened and the cooking liquid will be very red from the released cherry juice.

Take the mixture off the heat and cool slightly, then pour into a blender and blend just long enough to separate the pits from the cherries, no more than 30 seconds. Set a fine-mesh sieve over a large bowl, pour in the cherries, and press with a ladle to extract the liquid. Cool the syrup completely, and store in a sealed glass jar in the refrigerator for up to 1 month.

cardamom coffee

In Iran, coffee is known as ghahveh Turk, *or Turkish coffee, because it's prepared and drunk in the Turkish style: sweet, dark, and thick with coffee grounds. Like Persian tea, Persian coffee is often flavored with cardamom. Try adding cardamom to your morning brew—the combination of peppery-sweet cardamom with bitter coffee (or black tea) is simply sublime, especially when topped off with a splash of milk or cream. I recommend starting out with just $^1/_4$ teaspoon of cardamom per cup, but you can boost the flavor by adding more.*

serves 1

1 tablespoon whole or ground coffee beans

3 whole cardamom pods, or $^1/_4$ teaspoon ground cardamom

6 ounces hot water

If you're starting with whole coffee beans, combine the coffee beans and cardamom pods in a coffee grinder and grind finely. If you're starting with ground coffee, combine the coffee with the ground cardamom.

Brew the coffee as you normally would. Add milk or sweetener, if desired, or pour over ice.

Coffee, A Heavenly Brew

Although tea is the preferred hot beverage in Iran, coffee was once as popular there as it is throughout the West today, consumed liberally and propagated through a lively culture of coffeehouses that gave Persian men a place to assemble and exchange ideas. Coffee first appeared in Iran some time between the thirteenth and fifteenth centuries, reportedly discovered by a sheikh of the Sufi Muslim faith who had sampled it while traveling in Ethiopia, where coffee originates. Noting its energizing effects, he brought it north to Yemen to aid the Sufi mystics in their marathon whirling dervish dances, and from there its appeal spread to Sufi communities in Iran and throughout the Middle East. Over time, coffee would be widely embraced by secular Persians as well, and even praised by doctors for its medicinal uses. Coffee remained immensely popular until black tea—easier to source from nearby China and to cultivate locally—became Iran's eye-opener of choice in the nineteenth century.

naturally sweet dried lime tea

When I first tasted this lime-scented tea in an Arabic restaurant in Brooklyn, I couldn't get over how sweet it was, though the server insisted that there was absolutely no sugar in it. He was right: the tea is naturally sweetened by the dried limes. Lime tea is very refreshing served over ice, which gives it a more mild, diluted flavor, but I like to drink it hot, too. If you find the flavor too intense, just dilute the tea with more water. It also makes a deliciously bittersweet addition to cocktails. Use it much as you would lime juice or lemonade in cocktails like a margarita or a gimlet.

makes 8 cups

4 dried limes
1 cup hot water
7 cups cold water
Ice cubes (optional)

Soak the limes in the hot water for 15 minutes. Drain off the water into a pot. Add the cold water and bring to a boil.

Pierce the limes several times with a fork, or make incisions in them with a paring knife. Add the limes to the boiling water and simmer, covered, for 20 minutes. The water will turn a very subtle green from the limes. Press the limes against the side of the pot to extract as much liquid and flavor as possible, then remove. Drink the tea warm or serve over ice.

winter orchard tea

A jar of quince and orange tea is like a miniature garden. Close your eyes and take a deep breath of its honeyed bouquet and be transported to a lush, blooming oasis. Intoxicating rose petals make this tea distinctly Persian—an inspiration from my friend Nini, whose Tay Tea line boasts a blend called Persian Rose—while the cloves conjure the sweet scent of Christmas. Make this tea in winter, when quinces and oranges are in season, by simply drying the peels. Mix the blend with black tea leaves for a bittersweet, caffeinated boost. To serve, place about 2 teaspoons of the tea in a small tea ball and steep it in a mug of hot water for 3 to 5 minutes.

makes 2 cups tea mix

---

3 oranges
2 quinces
1 tablespoon dried rose petals or
    dried whole rosebuds pulled
    apart and stems removed

5 whole cloves
$^1/_4$ to $^1/_2$ cup black tea leaves,
    depending on your taste
    (optional)

Scrub the fruits and dry them thoroughly. Using a vegetable peeler, peel the oranges carefully so that only the orange part of the rind is removed, and not the bitter white part. Cut the quinces into thin strips, all the way down to the core, using the entire fruit.

Lay the orange peel and quince shavings on a cooling rack, screen, or baking sheet, and dry for 48 hours in a warm place, like the stove top. Mix the orange peels and quince with the rose petals and cloves. If you want a caffeinated tea, add the black tea leaves to the mix. Store in an airtight glass container at room temperature.

watermelon, mint, and cider vinegar tonic

sekanjabin

This refreshing mixture of nourishing cider vinegar and juicy watermelon is restorative and hydrating on a hot day. The mixture of vinegar and sugar is a time-honored Persian sharbat, or fruit essence drink, that's also used for dipping crisp romaine lettuce leaves in warm weather, another distinctly Persian way to hydrate. Just put a bowl of this beverage alongside a plate of romaine leaves and that's it: your salad is complete! Use raw, unfiltered cider vinegar to complement the taste of the watermelon.

makes 5 cups concentrate, enough for twenty 1-cup servings of tonic

3 cups water, plus more to serve
$^1/_4$ teaspoon sea salt
1 cup good-quality honey
6 cups coarsely chopped watermelon

1 cup tightly packed fresh spearmint
1 cup cider vinegar
Ice cubes

Sliced watermelon, sliced unwaxed cucumber, and spearmint, for garnish

Bring the 3 cups water and the salt to a boil in a medium saucepan. Add the honey, stir to dissolve, and remove from the heat.

Combine the watermelon and mint in a large bowl. Stir in the honey-water and let cool to room temperature, then add the vinegar. Steep the mixture in the refrigerator for several hours or up to overnight.

Strain the mixture and eat the watermelon chunks, if desired. Pour the concentrate into a clean glass jar, and store in the refrigerator for up to 1 week. To serve, pour $^1/_4$ cup of the concentrate into a glass over ice and dilute with $^3/_4$ cup water. Garnish with the watermelon, cucumber, and mint.

pickles and preserves

Evoking the legendary "walled gardens" of ancient Persia, the shelves of Persian grocery stores are lined with brilliantly colored bottles of preserves, from date molasses and bitter orange jam to grape syrup and carob paste. Meanwhile, the pickle section is full of strange concoctions like garlic and tiny grapes in brine, or the crushed whirl of green, white, and orange that is *torshi*, the sharply acidic pickle mix of vegetables and herbs that's one of Iran's essential condiments. In the rose water aisle, you'll find fleets of gleaming glass bottles with bright pink, red, and green labels, as if announcing the fragrant flowers captured inside.

Persians have been pickling, canning, drying, and fermenting their harvests for millennia, in part out of sheer necessity and in part for pure gustatory pleasure. An arid land from time immemorial, Iran's agricultural prowess began in the sixth century BCE, when King Cyrus helped expand an already existing system of underground irrigation channels called *qanats*. These subterranean waterways transported millions of gallons of water from Iran's mountainous snow-fed aquifers out to the parched, virtually uninhabitable regions of Iran.

The result was what must have appeared to be a magical blossoming of lush fruit, vegetable, and flower gardens in the midst of the once-barren Iranian desert. These remarkable oases were dubbed *pairidaeza*, or "walled

175

gardens," and to this day our English word "paradise" is a living echo of their miraculous effect. Still, a desert is a desert, and the Persian penchant for pickling and preserving grew out of a clear need to quickly protect as much of this rare desert produce as possible.

To this day, Persian preserves and pickles boast many extraordinary concoctions, and what follows is a small selection using some of Iran's most exquisite ingredients. The Sour Cherry and Rose Preserves (page 185) lend breakfast or snack time a hint of flowery fragrance, and the sweet zing of the Tamarind Date Chutney (page 183) and Fig Mustard (page 182) scintillates on a salty cheese platter or in a sandwich. Garlic enthusiasts may want to munch on the Garlic and Sun-Dried Tomato Pickle (page 181) on its own, while the bracingly tart *Torshi* (page 178) is in a class by itself as a briny balance to a succulent Persian meal.

The following recipes may be canned as you would other pickles and jams, but most of them can be stored in the refrigerator for several months in either clean glass bowls with fitted rubber lids or in glass jars.

sour plum pickle

gojeh sabz

Perfectly round and pale green, sour plums make a crisp and tangy pickle. In Iran, these puckering fruits are pickled, cooked with meat to lend lightness to a stew, or eaten raw with nothing but a pinch of salt. You can find sour plums on the West Coast of the United States in April, and on the East Coast in May, but these pickles can be made with unripe plums of any variety. (See photo on page 174.)

makes 4 cups

8 ounces sour plums
$1/4$ cup dried mint
3 cloves garlic, crushed
1 cup white wine vinegar

3 tablespoons water
1 teaspoon kosher salt
$1/4$ cup maple syrup

With a fork, poke several holes in the plums so the pickling liquid can penetrate, and place them in a clean glass bowl.

Combine the mint, garlic, vinegar, water, kosher salt, and maple syrup in a saucepan and bring to a boil. Lower the heat and simmer for 1 minute, then pour the mixture over the plums. Let the pickles cool to room temperature, then cover and marinate in the refrigerator overnight.

The pickles are ready to eat the next day, but will keep in an airtight container in the refrigerator for 2 weeks.

mixed vegetable pickle

torshi

Many a national pickle—Korean kimchi, German sauerkraut—is so central to a country's cuisine that a meal seems incomplete without them, and that's certainly true of torshi. Torshi gets its earthy taste from ground golpar, or angelica seeds, and smoky nigella seeds, also called black onion seeds or kalonji. (See photo on page 180.)

makes 3 quarts

2 pounds eggplant
¹/₂ teaspoon sea salt
1 pound cauliflower florets,
    broken into small pieces
1 pound carrots, finely diced

About 1 cup tightly packed fresh
    tarragon
4 cloves garlic, minced
1 shallot, minced
2 tablespoons nigella seeds
2 tablespoons coriander seeds

1 teaspoon ground golpar
2 tablespoons dried mint
4¹/₄ cups white wine vinegar, plus
    more if needed
1 tablespoon kosher salt

Preheat the oven to 425°F. Line two baking sheets with parchment paper.

Peel the eggplant and cut into small dice. Spread on the baking sheets and sprinkle ¹/₄ teaspoon of the sea salt over each sheet. Bake, stirring gently every 10 minutes to prevent sticking, for 40 minutes, until the eggplant is very soft. Let cool to room temperature.

Combine the cauliflower, carrots, and eggplant in a large bowl. Crush the tarragon in your palms to bring out the flavor and coarsely chop. Add the tarragon, garlic, and shallot to the vegetables.

In a hot, dry skillet, toast the nigella and coriander seeds for 30 seconds, then transfer to a plate to cool. Add the seeds, *golpar*, and mint to the vegetables, and mix well. Place the vegetables in a large, clean glass bowl with a fitted rubber lid or in glass jars.

Pour the vinegar into a large bowl. Add the kosher salt and whisk to dissolve, then pour over the vegetables to cover them completely. Add more vinegar to cover if necessary. Seal with the lid and store in the refrigerator. The pickles will be ready to eat in 2 weeks and will last for about 6 months in the refrigerator.

turnip and beet pickle

You'll find versions of this bright pink pickle throughout Middle Eastern cuisine. Tucked into flatbread, it makes a crisp and tangy addition to hot sandwiches, like the Potato Cakes with Tamarind Sauce (page 81) or the Sweet and Smoky Beet Burgers (page 79). These pickles are very tasty after 3 weeks, and even better after 6 weeks. (See photo on page 180.)

makes about 2 quarts

2 cups water
1 tablespoon kosher salt
2 tablespoons honey

1 cup white wine vinegar, plus more if needed
1 1/2 pounds red beets, peeled

1 pound turnips or rutabagas, peeled
4 cloves garlic, crushed

Heat the water to boiling. Add the salt and honey and whisk to dissolve. Turn off the heat and let cool to room temperature. Stir in the vinegar.

Slice the beets and turnips into thin French-fry batons, about 1/4 inch wide. Place the beets, turnips, and garlic in a large, clean glass bowl that has a fitted rubber lid or in glass jars.

Pour the pickling liquid over the vegetables. Add more vinegar to cover if necessary, then seal with a lid and refrigerate. The pickles will be ready to eat in 3 weeks and will last for about 6 months in the refrigerator.

Clockwise from left:
Turnip and Beet Pickle (page 179),
Tamarind Date Chutney (page 183),
Mixed Vegetable Pickle (page 178),
Fig Mustard (page 182), Garlic
and Sun-Dried Tomato Pickle
(opposite)

garlic and sun-dried tomato pickle

torsh-e sir

Pickled garlic is an Iranian delicacy. Aged as long as five, ten, even twenty-five years, the longer the garlic is pickled, the more precious it is. The samples I've tasted are pickled simply in red wine vinegar, but this bright, crisp condiment benefits from the addition of sun-dried tomatoes and a splash of sweet honey. Multiply this recipe as many times as you like. Use 1/2 teaspoon each of salt and sugar for every cup of vinegar that's used. For the best results, use young, fresh, unblemished garlic. (See photo opposite.)

makes 1 cup

1 head garlic, separated into cloves
1 or 2 dry-packed sun-dried tomatoes, torn

$^1/_2$ teaspoon organic cane sugar
1 tablespoon honey
$^1/_2$ teaspoon kosher salt
Red wine vinegar, to cover

Prepare a bowl of ice water and bring a small saucepan of water to a boil. Drop the garlic into the boiling water and boil for 2 minutes, then drain and immediately immerse in the ice water. When cool, pull off the skins. Slice off any brown or broken spots, and place the garlic in a clean glass pint jar.

Add the sun-dried tomatoes to the garlic, followed by the sugar, honey, and kosher salt. Add vinegar to cover, seal, and shake to dissolve the sugar, honey, and salt. Label the jar with the date and store it in the refrigerator.

The pickles are tasty within a few days but will be really flavorful in 2 weeks. When serving, remove portions with a clean spoon. The pickles will last for about 6 months in the refrigerator and acquire a more intense flavor with time.

fig mustard

Half mustard and half jam, this sweet and spicy fig spread is textured with tiny, supple fig seeds that tease the tongue. Its pungent fruit essence complements a platter of rich cheese and lends a sweet acidity to sandwiches and salad dressings. Toasting the mustard seeds helps to bring their flavor to life, but just 30 seconds is plenty of time—they can burn quickly. Use either a mortar and pestle or a spice grinder to coarsely grind the mustard seeds. (See photo on page 180.)

makes about 1½ cups

8 ounces dried figs, stemmed
    and halved
1 cup water, boiling
½ cup mustard seeds

1 tablespoon kosher salt
1 cup organic cane sugar
½ cup freshly squeezed lemon
    juice

Combine the figs and water in a small saucepan. Return to a boil, then cover and simmer for 5 minutes.

Meanwhile, in a hot, dry skillet, toast the mustard seeds for 30 seconds, then quickly transfer to a plate to stop the cooking. When cool, grind the mustard into powder. Add the mustard to the figs and cook over low heat for 5 minutes, stirring occasionally. The mixture should be bubbling gently.

Transfer the figs to a food processor and pulse until smooth. Return the figs to the saucepan and place over medium-high heat. Add the sugar and lemon juice and bring to a boil, stirring continually, until the mixture comes to a boil and the sugar dissolves. Let cool to room temperature.

Transfer to a clean glass jar and let cool completely. Seal with a lid and refrigerate. The spread is ready to eat right away and will last for about 6 months in the refrigerator.

tamarind date chutney

torshi-e khorma

This sublime condiment brings together tamarind, lime, ginger, cinnamon, and sugary dates. Once pickled in the tamarind, the dates crystallize and dissolve into a soft paste similar to a chutney. After 6 weeks, the pronounced salty flavor of the sumac will mellow, and you can enjoy this fragrant pickle on everything from burgers to fish to cheese. For an easy hors d'oeuvre, spread it on a cracker and top it with lime powder–seasoned grilled shrimp (page 87) and a fresh green herb. The chutney will separate slightly over time, so stir it from the bottom before serving to bring out all its tart lime goodness. (See photo on page 180.)

makes about 3 cups

1 cup Thai tamarind concentrate (see page 16), strained to remove grit
1/3 cup freshly squeezed lime juice, plus more if needed

2 tablespoons sumac
1 teaspoon kosher salt
2 cloves garlic, minced
1-inch piece fresh ginger, peeled and minced

1/2 teaspoon ground cinnamon
1 pound Medjool dates, pitted

In a large bowl, whisk the tamarind with the lime juice, sumac, kosher salt, garlic, ginger, and cinnamon. Add the dates and toss well.

Transfer the mixture to a clean glass jar and add more lime juice as needed to cover any exposed dates. Seal and store in the refrigerator. Shake every few days to break up the crystallization. The dates will be ready to eat in 6 weeks and will last for about 6 months in the refrigerator.

sour cherry and rose preserves

moraba-ye albalu

This refreshingly tart jam is scented with rose water and vanilla. Cooking the jam in a deep skillet helps the liquid evaporate much faster than in a pot, but be careful: the preserves will thicken in a matter of minutes and can become too thick to spread if allowed to overcook. The jam should cook no longer than 10 to 12 minutes, even if it seems thin, as it will thicken dramatically as it cools. Spread the preserves on scones and muffins, heat them with a little water to make a thick syrup for glazing meat and poultry, or use in place of fresh sour cherries in the Rice with Sour Cherries and Almonds recipe (page 134).

makes 2 cups

1 pound sour cherries
1 1/2 cups organic cane sugar
1 tablespoon rose water

1 teaspoon vanilla extract
1 tablespoon freshly squeezed
   lime juice

Stem and pit the cherries. Heat the cherries in a large, deep skillet over medium-high heat. When the cherries start to bubble, add the sugar and bring to a boil. Lower the heat to a gentle boil and stir constantly to dissolve the sugar and prevent the mixture from burning. Boil for 10 to 12 minutes, until the cherries start to shrink and the liquid thickens. Although the mixture may not look as thick as finished jam, it will thicken when it cools, so be sure to stop cooking after 12 minutes. Stir in the rose water, vanilla, and lime juice and turn off the heat.

Pour the preserves into clean glass jars and let cool to room temperature, then seal and refrigerate. The preserves will keep for up to 1 year in the refrigerator.

Menus

SUMMER BARBECUE

Chile-Saffron Fish Kebabs (*Kebab-e Mahi*) • page 85
Chicken Kebabs in Yogurt Marinade (*Joojeh Kebab*) • page 100
Fresh Herb Platter (*Sabzi Khordan*) • page 27
Persian-Style Grilled Corn (*Balal*) • page 30
Rice with Sour Cherries and Almonds (*Albalu Polo*) • page 134
Saffron Frozen Yogurt and Cardamom Pizzelle Sandwiches (*Bastani*) • page 151
Sour Cherry Spritzer • page 168

MIDSUMMER DINNER, TIRGAN DINNER

Cold Pistachio Soup with Mint and Leeks • page 41
Seared Chicken with Peaches (*Khoresh-e Hulu*) • page 112
Saffron Rice • page 123
Roasted Stuffed Artichokes with Mint Oil • page 73
Mulberry Yogurt Cake • page 153
Watermelon, Mint, and Cider Vinegar Tonic (*Sekanjabin*) • page 173

PERSIAN GULF—INSPIRED TROPICAL LUNCH

Roasted Peach and Corn Salad in Tamarind Vinaigrette • page 61
Grilled Shrimp with Lime Powder and Parsley–Olive Oil Sauce • page 87
Tomato Rice with Dried Limes (*Estamboli Polo*) • page 137

EID UL-FITR DINNER

Fresh Herb Platter (*Sabzi Khordan*) • page 27
Cold Pistachio Soup with Mint and Leeks (*Soup-e Pesteh*) • page 41
Potato Cakes with Tamarind Sauce (*Kotlet*) • page 81
Turmeric Chicken with Sumac and Lime • page 103
Sweet Rice with Carrots and Nuts (*Shirin Polo*) • page 125
Date-and-Walnut-Filled Cookies (*Koloocheh*) • page 155
Date Shake with Toasted Nuts (*Majoon*) • page 167

SHABBAT DINNER

Fresh Herb Platter (*Sabzi Khordan*) • page 27
Eggplant and Tomato Stew with Pomegranate Molasses (*Bademjan*) • page 107
Rice with Rose Petals and Barberries • page 127
Chickpea and Almond Flour Icebox Cookies (*Nan-e Nokhodchi*) • page 145
Fresh fruit

THANKSGIVING DINNER, *MEHREGAN* DINNER

Fresh Herb Platter (*Sabzi Khordan*) • page 27

Pomegranate Walnut Stew (*Fesenjan*) • page 109

Sweet Rice with Carrots and Nuts (*Shirin Polo*) • page 125

Yogurt with Beets (*Borani Chogondar*) • page 35

Winter Squash Fritters with Rose Petals • page 28

No-Bake Persimmon and Goat Cheese Cheesecake • page 159

Fresh seasonal fruit, including pomegranates and apples

CHRISTMAS OR HANNUKAH DINNER, *SHAB-E YALDA* DINNER

Shaved Celery Root and Pomegranate Salad • page 60

Lamb Meatballs with Mint and Garlic (*Kufteh*) • page 88

Parvin's Tamarind Stuffed Fish • page 90

Jeweled Brown Basmati Rice and Quinoa (*Morassa Polo*) • page 121

Yogurt with Shallots (*Mast-o Musir*) • page 36

Pomegranate Semifreddo with Blood Orange Compote • page 148

CLASSIC KEBAB MEAL

Lamb Kebabs in Pomegranate-Walnut Marinade (*Kebab-e Torsh*) • page 95

Saffron Rice (*Chelo*) • page 123

Fresh Herb Platter (*Sabzi Khordan*) • page 27

Salty Mint Yogurt Soda (*Doogh*) • page 165

Mixed Vegetable Pickle (*Torshi*) • page 178

Yogurt with Shallots (*Mast-o Musir*) • page 36

EASY WEEKNIGHT DINNER

Turmeric Chicken with Sumac and Lime • page 103

Saffron Rice (*Chelo*) • page 123

Tomato and Cucumber Salad (*Salad Shirazi*) • page 59

Resources

ONLINE STORES FOR
GENERAL PERSIAN
INGREDIENTS

Kalamala
www.kalamala.com

Kalustyan's
*Persian ingredients, as well as
Thai tamarind concentrate*
www.kalustyans.com

Sadaf
www.sadaf.com

Shahrzad
www.shahrzad.com

ONLINE STORES FOR
OTHER SELECT GOODS

C. Palmer Manufacturing
Company
*Pizzelle maker, Model 3000;
makes three 3-inch round
pizzelles*
www.cpalmermfg.com

Cayuga Pure Organics
*Organically grown beans,
flours, and whole grains*
www.cporganics.com

Grocery Thai
Thai tamarind concentrate
www.grocerythai.com

Penzey's
For spices
www.penzeys.com

Tavazo Dried Nuts & Fruits
(949) 552-7780
*Iranian specialty store for
dried nuts and fruits; contact
via email*
simatavazo@yahoo.ca

You can find a listing of
local markets that carry
Persian ingredients at
www.lucidfood.com.

BOOKS ON OR ABOUT
PERSIAN FOOD

Batmanglij, Najmieh. *Food
of Life: Ancient Persian and
Modern Iranian Cooking and
Ceremonies*. Washington, DC:
Mage Publishers, 2011.
Bijan, Donia. *Maman's Homesick
Pie*. Chapel Hill, NC:
Algonquin Books, 2011.

Ghanoonparvar, M. R. *Persian
Cuisine: Traditional, Regional,
and Modern Foods*. Costa
Mesa, CA: Mazda, 2006.
Malouf, Greg, and Lucy Malouf.
*Saraban: A Chef's Journey
Through Persia*. Victoria,
Australia: Hardie Grant Books,
2011.
Marks, Gil. *Encyclopedia of Jewish
Food*. Hoboken, NJ: Wiley,
2010.
Mazda, Maideh. *In a Persian
Kitchen*. Rutland, VT: Tuttle,
1989.
Shaida, Margaret. *The Legendary
Cuisine of Persia*. Oxfordshire,
UK: Lieuse Publications, 1992.
Simnegar, Reyna. *Persian Food
from the Non-Persian Bride*.
Jerusalem: Philipp Feldheim,
2011.

BOOKS ON PERSIAN
CULTURE

Dumas, Firoozeh. *Funny in
Farsi: A Memoir of Growing Up
Iranian in America*. New York:
Random House, 2004.

Elliot, Jason. *Mirrors of the Unseen*. New York: St. Martin's Press, 2006.

Ferdowsi, Abolqasem, and Dick Davis. *The Shahnameh*. Washington, DC: Mage Publishers, 1997.

Moridani, Bijan. *The Persian Wedding*. Tarzana, CA: Inner Layers, 2005.

Mottahedeh, Roy. *The Mantle of the Prophet: Religion and Politics in Iran*. Oxford, UK: Oneworld, 2008.

Nafishi, Azar. *Reading Lolita in Tehran*. New York: Random House, 2003.

Satrapi, Marjane. *Persepolis: The Story of a Childhood*. Paris: L'Association, Pantheon, 2003.

Sciolino, Elaine. *Persian Mirrors*. New York: Free Press, 2005.

Acknowledgments

The essence of this book comes from my extended family, who taught me as much about generosity as they did about food. Mahin Shafieha and Hossein Taherizadegan took me home and taught me how to make *baghali polo* and *nan-e panjere'i*. Shirin Khamessi, Iraj, Sanam, and Samar Javid took me to Southern California's best Persian markets, cooked me beautiful food, and unearthed family history for me. Ali Hajimiri and Roshanak Shafiiha prepared a New Year's Day feast that felt like a homecoming, Reyhanak Shafiiha introduced me to *abgoosht* and the meaning of rose water, and Parvin Dabir shared with me her recipe for *Norooz* fish. With the wonderful feasts she prepared during my childhood, Meliheh Shafiiha helped provide the inspiration for this book.

I'm grateful for the help of Mehrnoush Soroush with Persian translation, and for connecting me with Somayeh Yousefi, Shokouh Pooraryan, and Mahyar Pooraryan, who spent long days teaching me about Persian cooking and culture and feeding me delectable homemade food. Thanks to Nini Ordoubadi and Anna Fahr for inspiration and support. I can't thank my wonderful recipe testers Raquel Dorman, Rachel Hannon, Nellie Kurtzman, Aimee Martinez, Trey Popp, Joy Rotondi, and Michelle Warner enough for their honesty and insights.

I'm lucky to continue to work with the very wise Michael Psaltis. My great appreciation likewise goes to my editor, Sara Golski, for her smart questions and observations. Thanks to Sara Remington, Ethel Brennan, and Karen Shinto for crafting the luscious look of the photos, and to Toni Tajima for her unparalleled abilities in designing the book. I can't imagine working with a better team.

Finally, I want to thank James Rotondi for his love and support throughout the writing of this book, from accompanying me on research trips to Turkey and Los Angeles, to enthusiastically sampling all fourteen versions of *koolocheh*, to embracing Persian culture and becoming a member of my family in spirit as well as on paper. I look forward to all of our adventures to come.

About the Author

*L*ouisa Shafia's first cookbook, *Lucid Food: Cooking for an Eco-Conscious Life*, was nominated for an IACP award. She has cooked at notable restaurants in New York and San Francisco, including Aquavit, Pure Food and Wine, and Millennium. Her recipes have appeared in *New York* magazine, *Yoga Journal*, *Food Network Magazine*, and *Every Day with Rachael Ray*. Look for Louisa on the Cooking Channel's Taste in Translation series, and visit her at www.lucidfood.com.

Index

Persian rugs courtesy The Oriental Carpet, Menlo Park, California www.theorientalcarpet.com

Library of Congress Cataloging-in-Publication Data
Shafia, Louisa.
   The new Persian kitchen / Louisa Shafia ; photography by Sara Remington. —First edition.
      pages cm
   Includes index.
   1. Cooking, Iranian. I. Title.
   TX725.I7S38 2013
   641.5953—dc23

                                    2012038828

ISBN 978-1-60774-357-6
eISBN 978-1-60774-358-3

Printed in China

Design by Toni Tajima
Food styling by Karen Shinto
Prop styling by Ethel Brennan
Food styling assistance by Jeffrey Larsen

10 9 8 7 6 5 4 3 2 1

First Edition

MEASUREMENT CONVERSION CHARTS

VOLUME

U.S.	IMPERIAL	METRIC
1 tablespoon	$1/2$ fl oz	15 ml
2 tablespoons	1 fl oz	30 ml
$1/4$ cup	2 fl oz	60 ml
$1/3$ cup	3 fl oz	90 ml
$1/2$ cup	4 fl oz	120 ml
$2/3$ cup	5 fl oz ($1/4$ pint)	150 ml
$3/4$ cup	6 fl oz	180 ml
1 cup	8 fl oz ($1/3$ pint)	240 ml
$1 1/4$ cups	10 fl oz ($1/2$ pint)	300 ml
2 cups (1 pint)	16 fl oz ($2/3$ pint)	480 ml
$2 1/2$ cups	20 fl oz (1 pint)	600 ml
1 quart	32 fl oz ($1 2/3$ pints)	1 l

TEMPERATURE

FAHRENHEIT	CELSIUS/GAS MARK
250°F	120°C/gas mark $1/2$
275°F	135°C/gas mark 1
300°F	150°C/gas mark 2
325°F	160°C/gas mark 3
350°F	180 or 175°C/gas mark 4
375°F	190°C/gas mark 5
400°F	200°C/gas mark 6
425°F	220°C/gas mark 7
450°F	230°C/gas mark 8
475°F	245°C/gas mark 9
500°F	260°C

LENGTH

INCH	METRIC
$1/4$ inch	6 mm
$1/2$ inch	1.25 cm
$3/4$ inch	2 cm
1 inch	2.5 cm
6 inches ($1/2$ foot)	15 cm
12 inches (1 foot)	30 cm

WEIGHT

U.S./IMPERIAL	METRIC
$1/2$ oz	15 g
1 oz	30 g
2 oz	60 g
$1/4$ lb	115 g
$1/3$ lb	150 g
$1/2$ lb	225 g
$3/4$ lb	350 g
1 lb	450 g